Training Spirit-Filled
Local Church Leaders
for the
Twenty-First Century

Training Spirit-Filled Local Church Leaders

for the

Twenty-First Century

RAY MILLER

RESOURCE *Publications* · Eugene, Oregon

Resource Publications
An Imprint of Wipf and Stock Publishers
199 W. 8th Ave., Suite 3
Eugene, OR 97401

www.wipfandstock.com

PAPERBACK ISBN: 978-1-6667-1568-2
HARDCOVER ISBN: 978-1-6667-1569-9
EBOOK ISBN: 978-1-6667-1570-5

AUGUST 18, 2021

To Deborah

Contents

Unit 3: Training

Unit 4: The Twenty-First Century

Tables

Introduction

It will come about after this that I will pour out My Spirit on all mankind; And your sons and daughters will prophesy, your old men will dream dreams, your young men will see visions. Even on the male and female servants I will pour out My Spirit in those days.

Joel 2:28–29

It is a trustworthy statement: if any man aspires to the office of overseer, it is a fine work he desires to do. An overseer, then, must be above reproach, the husband of one wife, temperate, prudent, respectable, hospitable, able to teach, not addicted to wine or pugnacious, but gentle, peaceable, free from the love of money. He must be one who manages his own household well, keeping his children under control with all dignity (but if a man does not know how to manage his own household, how will he take care of the church of God?), and not a new convert, so that he will not become conceited and fall into the condemnation incurred by the devil. And he must have a good reputation with those outside the church, so that he will not fall into reproach and the snare of the devil.

1 Tim 3:1–7

The things which you have heard from me in the presence of many witnesses, entrust these to faithful men who will be able to teach others also.

2 Tim 2:2

THESE BIBLICAL PASSAGES, INSPIRED by the Holy Spirit, express the heart of this book. I believe three foundational truths about the fulfillment of Christ's Great Commission. First, believers can fulfill the Great Commission only through the Spirit's constant guidance and empowerment. Second, this calling can be advanced only through healthy local churches present and actively involved in their communities. Third, those churches must have Spirit-filled leaders who invest themselves in the emerging generation of leaders.

I can identify several strategic moments and seasons that led to the writing of this book. One was a prayer retreat in 1987. During that time, I sensed that God was calling me to involvement with ministerial training. Although my assumption at that time was that I would teach at a Bible school in the U.S., life did not take me in that direction.

Later, on my first short-term ministry trip to the Philippines in 1996, my guide and interpreter was a denominational leader on the island where I was doing ministry. After teaching at a Bible school in Puerto Princesa, Palawan, the two of us traveled throughout the northern part of the island to minister in several rural churches. One of the congregations had no pastor, and our conversation about the needs of that church quickly moved to the question of how to provide one for them. It was unlikely that any current Bible school student would move there to lead the congregation after completing his or her studies. Thus, the most realistic possibility for that situation was someone from that congregation sensing a call to lead it.

After discussing this need, the leader and I began to think together about how to train such a person and encourage him or her to take up this challenging responsibility. That conversation became an important moment in the process that the Holy Spirit used to confirm my call to serve as a missionary in the Philippines. For fifteen years (2002–2017), I invested myself primarily in training pastors and other local church leaders. That conversation in 1996 and my experiences as a missionary spurred a renewed interest in and passion for ministerial training, with a desire to research and write about it. That culminated in my doing a Doctor of Ministry degree at Asia Pacific Theological Seminary in Baguio City, Philippines, and then this writing project.

Throughout the twentieth century, ministerial training was an essential part of the worldwide growth of the Assemblies of God[1] and other Pentecostal and charismatic groups. As the twenty-first century progresses,

1 McGee, *This Gospel*, 199.

churches and movements embracing the contemporary work of the Holy Spirit will need to continue to provide training to new generations of leaders. The challenge is to offer effective training and deliver it in new ways while maintaining a dependence on and sensitivity to the Spirit.

I write from the perspective of an Assemblies of God minister. At the same time, I recognize that many commonalities exist between Pentecostals, charismatics, third wavers, and many others who embrace the active, dynamic work of the Holy Spirit in the church and in the world today. Thus, I desire that all who have a passion for the training of Spirit-filled leaders for the local church and who study this book will receive encouragement, affirmation, insight, and inspiration for Spirit-led innovation that will sharpen their training ministry to those called by God to lead the local church.

I do not write this from the perspective of a theologian, at least as theologians are perceived in the popular mind. I write from the perspective of someone who has studied at institutions in North America and Asia. My concern is not for the kind of precision or length of discussion that might impress academics. It is for the continued health of the local church and for the ability of every generation of disciples that populates it to fulfill its God-given mandate to advance the Great Commission.

This book is not intended as an exhaustive discussion of Spirit-filled ministerial training nor as the last word on the subject. Rather, use it first as a handbook to provide a broad catalogue of various ideas about the topic. Let it stimulate prayer, thought, and discussion on a subject of extreme importance to the future of God's work in the world.

I have organized the units based on the title of the book: *Training Spirit-Filled Local Church Leaders for the Twenty-First Century*. That is the rationale for the organization of the book: "The Church," "Spiritual Leadership," "Training," and "The Twenty-First Century."

Although one can gain the most benefit by reading the entire book, each chapter can serve as a stand-alone essay. Admittedly, overlap in the topics exists in places. Where appropriate, I reference related information from other areas of the book in the footnotes.

I use the word training because it reflects the most common term for theological education among my anticipated audience, though training can unfortunately create a mental picture of ministry as simply a profession for which one learns skills to succeed or increase effectiveness. I have studiously avoided words like production (implying that ministry schools produce spiritual leaders) and other terms that reflect a mechanistic image.

My preferred term for ministry training is formation, although for some people, this term may not seem comprehensive enough. Interestingly, when Jesus called Simon and Andrew (Matt 4:19; Mark 1:17), the root of the term he used (*poieo*) when he promised to make them fishers of men can refer to work of a creative nature.[2] Educators taking a cue from Christ's wording here see themselves working cooperatively with the Holy Spirit to form the lives of their students to become spiritual leaders in the same way that Jesus formed his chosen apostles.

May Jesus Christ, Lord of the harvest, use the contents of this book, imperfect as they and its author are, to advance his saving and redeeming purposes in our world, and may he be exalted through it.

2 Braun, "Poieo."

Unit 1: The Church

Chapter 1

The Church and the Holy Spirit

INTRODUCTION

IF WE DESIRE TO understand how to train leaders for the local church, it is necessary to first understand the universal church. The overarching topic of this book addresses the training of Spirit-filled leaders for the local church, so the emphasis in this chapter will be the local congregation, with special stress on the pneumatological aspects of the universal church.

There are contrasts between the local church, the universal church, and the kingdom of God. The kingdom of God is more encompassing than the church locally or universally and refers essentially to the settings throughout history where God's rule or reign is embraced, along with the accompanying blessings.[1] The church is the gathering together of God's people either in a local setting or universally (chronologically and geographically), although in practical terms, the New Testament (NT) seems to emphasize the local assembly of believers.[2]

The Spirit provides the dynamic power for the advancement of God's mission throughout the world and guides the process as the church crosses cultural, geographic, ethnic, and linguistic borders to carry out God's

---

1. See Elwell and Comfort, "Kingdom of God, Kingdom of Heaven," in *Tyndale Bible Dictionary*, 776–78.

2. See Robinson, "Church," 199–202.

mission in the world.[3] The Spirit also continues to work within established churches as they serve within their immediate communities.

THE PURPOSE OF THE CHURCH

God's mission in the world can be summed up as the reconciliation of humans to God.[4] The essence of the Great Commission in the Gospels and Acts is holistic in the sense that the church is to proclaim the gospel and form disciples. This task—consisting of proclamation, establishing local congregations into which believers are to be assimilated, and transformational teaching (making disciples)—is to be done through the empowerment and guidance of the Holy Spirit.

In fulfilling this mission, the church can be understood as having a fourfold means to accomplish it.[5] Rather than being a social entity that exists for itself, it is created by Christ and empowered by the Spirit for the benefit of the world around it. The four aspects of its purpose are evangelism, worship, edification, and social responsibility. Each of these aspects is interrelated to the other three, and all are essential to the ultimate purpose of the local church in fulfilling the Great Commission.

SPIRIT ECCLESIOLOGY

Keith Warrington describes the local Pentecostal church as existing and functioning with a "Spirit ecclesiology."[6] One area that reveals to what extent Spirit ecclesiology is a reality is the practical interaction between the universal church and God's mission. The church should properly be seen as a direct participant in God's mission, rather than existing apart from it or in a way that is not organically integrated into God's mission in the world.[7] Miguel Alvarez explains that

---

3. See Klaus, "Mission of the Church," 574–81.

4. See Klaus, "Mission of the Church," 567–68. There are other views of this from various theological perspectives, but reconciliation of humans to God is the focus of this book. See Pomerville, *Third Force in Missions*, 137–43.

5. See Dusing, "New Testament Church," 543–45.

6. Warrington, *Pentecostal Theology*, 134.

7. See Alvarez, "Distinctives of Pentecostal Education," 286; Duraisingh, "Ministerial Formation for Mission," 33–45.

mission is not one among many functions of the Church, instead the Church is a function of God's mission. If the Church is the instrument and expression of the kingdom, then the goal of theological education is to form people in congregations so that they can participate in God's local and global mission.[8]

The Spirit works in and through the church to motivate, empower, and guide God's mission in the world. Although the mission may in some ways proceed independently from the church through parachurch organizations or other means, a local church's reason for being must not be separated from its direct involvement in fulfilling God's mission.

THE SPIRIT'S WORK IN THE CHURCH

The work of the Spirit is Christocentric.[9] In his farewell discourse to the disciples, Jesus promised that the Spirit would abide with them and represent him (John 14:16–17), be sent to them in Jesus's name to teach them (John 14:26), testify to them and through them about Jesus (John 15:26–27), and convict the unbelieving world of the truth and guide the disciples into the truth (John 16:8–15).

Jesus promised that the Spirit would come and empower the disciples specifically to be witnesses to him (Acts 1:8). The Spirit began to be poured out on the Day of Pentecost by the resurrected and ascended Jesus (Acts 2:32–33). The Spirit emboldened Peter to proclaim Jesus as the one and only way of salvation (Acts 4:8–12).

Only through the influence of the Holy Spirit can one confess Jesus as Lord (1 Cor 12:3). The Spirit is intimately involved in the salvation experience as the new believer trusts in Christ (Eph 1:13; Titus 3:5). The Spirit is directly involved in the process of proclamation (1 Pet 1:12).

This Christocentric work of the Spirit continues and is a central factor in what happens at every level of the local congregation. The Spirit exalts Christ and moves his redemptive purposes forward in the life of each individual believer, in the leadership of the church, in the corporate life of the church as it advances God's redemptive purpose in its community, and as the local church participates globally in the advancement of God's redemptive purpose.

8. See Alvarez, "Distinctives of Pentecostal Education," 286.

9. Boer, *Pentecost and Missions*, 110–12, 130–34; Horton, *What the Bible Says*, 210–11.

The church is by nature a pneumatic and charismatic entity. It was created by the Holy Spirit, continues to be sustained and guided by the Spirit, and functions through the sovereign working of the Spirit in and through its members.[10]

There are several ways that the NT describes the relationship and interaction between the Spirit and the church. Following are some relevant ones.

The Church Is a Dwelling Place of the Spirit

The church is described as a temple of God in which the Spirit dwells (1 Cor 3:16–17; it should be noted that a similar phrase in 6:18–20 is a reference to the believer's physical body and not the church). The temple is the third in a series of metaphors in 1 Cor 3 about the church; it is God's garden (5–9) and God's building (10–15). This temple is special as an "inner sanctuary" of God[11] in which "the Spirit makes His home."[12] This is a reference specifically to the local congregation.[13]

The Church Operates in the Gifts of the Spirit

There are a vast variety of gifts,[14] all distributed by the sovereign determination of the Spirit.[15] The gifts and their manifestation always bring honor to Christ[16] and are given for the strengthening of the church.[17] The motivation behind the manifestation of the gifts is love.[18]

---

10. Kung, *Church*, 201–50.

11. Wuest, *New Testament*, 1 Cor 3:16.

12. Wuest, *New Testament*, 1 Cor 3:16.

13. See Lowery, "1 Corinthians," 2:511–12.

14. Horton, *What the Bible Says*, 209–10.

15. Horton, *What the Bible Says*, 213–14.

16. Horton, *What the Bible Says*, 211–13.

17. Horton, *What the Bible Says*, 224–28.

18. Horton, *What the Bible Says*, 219–21.

The Church Is Guided by the Spirit to Fulfill Its Purpose

The dynamic prophetic empowerment of the church and of believers for witness is a well-studied topic.[19] A related topic Luke seems to emphasize, but which may be less familiar to some, appears at strategic moments in Acts. This topic is the ability to solve problems that could hinder the fulfillment of God's redemptive purpose and to make decisions that in retrospect are shown to expedite its advance. Examples of this are the choosing of the Seven to assist the Jerusalem leaders (Acts 6:1–6), the sending of Peter and John to confirm the Samaritans' experience (Acts 8:14–17), the commissioning and sending of Barnabas and Saul (Acts 13:1–3), the decision of the Jerusalem Council affirming Peter's ministry to the household of Cornelius (Acts 15:22–29), and the decision to go northwest into Europe rather than further east into Asia Minor (Acts 16:6–10).

THE CHURCH IS BOTH AN ORGANISM AND ORGANIZATION

The church exists and functions simultaneously as a living organism and as an organizational structure.[20] Disagreements about whether it is an organism or an organization have been based on the assumption that it must be one or the other. Each way of understanding the church helps us to appreciate what it is and how it can most effectively fulfill its God-given purpose in the world.

The NT describes the church in organic terms, portraying it as the body of Christ (1 Cor 12:12–30) with parts that fulfill many different functions through the working of the Spirit in each part. This body builds itself up through the participation of each individual member (Eph 4:4–5, 12–16). The church also relates and responds collectively to Christ, its head (Eph 1:22–23; 5:23). These various individual and corporate perspectives reflect a dynamic and ongoing involvement of the Spirit in the life of the local church.

The NT also reflects a process of organizational development. As early as Acts 6, a ministry structure needed to be put in place. There was a practical need (v. 1) that had the potential of dividing the congregation and distracting the leadership (vv. 1–2). Leaders who were observably qualified

---

19. Stronstad, *Charismatic Theology*; Stronstad, *Spirit, Scripture, and Theology*.
20. See Dusing, "New Testament Church," 545–47.

were selected to carry out responsibilities (vv. 3–6). Immediately following this selection, Luke notes that "the word of God kept on spreading; and the number of the disciples continued to increase greatly in Jerusalem, and a great many of the priests were becoming obedient to the faith" (v. 7).

Pneumatic movements have existed throughout Church history.[21] There have been many reasons for those movements' disappearance or disintegration. One may have been a failure to utilize a sufficient level of organization, based on distrust or dislike of organization. As a result, it was impossible to perpetuate the movement.

The Spirit may at first glance seem to fit more with an organic view of the church. However, such a view would be unbalanced. The Spirit's involvement should be sought, welcomed, and embraced in both the organic and organizational aspects of church life.

The Spirit uses the local church and its ministry experiences to prepare disciples to participate in God's mission of reconciliation.[22] The local church should structure itself to send its members to reach outsiders (a *go* structure) and not just to invite outsiders to attend (a *come* structure).[23]

One example of structuring ministry in this way is seen in Latin American Pentecostal churches.[24] Believers, having been built up spiritually and instructed in practical terms, proclaim Christ to those around them using strategies such as street preaching. They then invite hearers to receive Christ. Those who receive Christ are immediately introduced to a local fellowship and encouraged to become a growing part of it.

CONCLUSION

While the local church tends to be understood through the lens of the traditional Western church model, such an expression of Christianity may not fit every cultural setting. John and Anita Koeshall describe five Anchoring Events that characterize what a community of Christian faith experiences together and that constitute being a church:

---

21. See Barrett, "Chronology of Renewal," 415–52.

22. See Klaus, "Mission of the Church," 586–94.

23. Lim, *Drama of Redemption*, 79–84.

24. Wagner, *Spiritual Power and Church Growth*, 43–52. Although this information is somewhat dated, it reflects the ability to harness cultural practices for the purpose of advancing the Great Commission in an effective way.

1. They experience and respond to God's presence and the Lordship of Jesus through the working of the Holy Spirit among them;

2. They study, interpret, and apply God's word together for the purpose of being transformed by the Holy Spirit more into the image of Christ in every area of life;

3. All members of the community, no matter what their level of maturity, serve as the Spirit enables them, contributing to the process of the spiritual growth (discipleship) of the other members;

4. They see themselves as more than just redeemed individuals; they are a part of Christ's redeemed community that is being formed by the working of the Spirit;

5. Through the guidance, empowerment, passion, and equipping of the Spirit, they cooperate together to make Christ known and experienced by the community around them.[25]

Scripture clearly teaches about the dynamic and necessary relationship between the individual believer and the Holy Spirit. However, there is a great deal that can be missed, especially in individualistic cultures, about the work of the Spirit relative to the local congregation. It is equally vital to understand the work of the Spirit in the local congregation in a missional sense. Only by understanding these three dynamics—ecclesiology, pneumatology, and mission—in a vital and interconnected way can the church have a basis for providing the kind of spiritual leaders it needs for every century, including the twenty-first.

---

25. Koeshall and Koeshall, "Ecclesiology to Go," 5–13.

Chapter 2

The Church
and the Training Institution

INTRODUCTION

AN AREA RELATED TO the church and ministerial training that sometimes receives insufficient attention is the relationship between two primary entities: the church at the local and denominational level and the school. The importance of this relationship cannot be overstated. This topic is foundational to training because the future of local churches is strongly influenced by the training of the next generation of leaders.

This chapter advocates for a symbiotic partnership between the two institutions of church and school and briefly describes a few strategic areas where that partnership can be expressed. It also suggests ways the local church can provide opportunities for training.

SYMBIOTIC PARTNERSHIP

Keith Warrington argues for a symbiotic partnership to exist between the church and the school.[1] He appeals to Pentecostal educators:

> A symbiotic partnership needs to be strengthened between Colleges and church constituencies who send students there in order to maximise the learning process for all concerned, recognising

1. Warrington, *Pentecostal Theology*, 157.

the different emphases and expectations stressed by each. The fear of being marginalized from the training of future leaders should cause all involved in Pentecostal College education to reconsider that which they are offering and its relevance. The local church often functions as a hermeneutical context for the learning and practice of the student. It can provide the College with the knowledge as to whether it is providing that which the churches need; the Academy must never forget that it is the servant of the Church (not its replacement) and that as such, it must prove its value by helping the Church. Discussions between leaders of each institution therefore ought to take place regularly for the purposes of listening to each other, understanding each other's priorities and to celebrate the fact that God has gifted each to the other. Practical measures can be undertaken to facilitate support frameworks for the benefit of both; this demands time, patience and sensitivity but will ensure that they do not miss each other on the way. The danger otherwise is that there will be a clash of priorities without the opportunity to recognise the value of the emphases of both the Church and the Academy.[2]

The church and school can express this symbiotic, cooperative relationship through virtually every aspect of training, thus positively impacting each area. Cooperation between the church and training institution will flow from purposefully nurturing a mutual understanding, appreciation, and support for what each entity brings to the training ministry. This cooperative spirit should entail a natural, organic expression of a servanthood and partnership orientation toward ministry. A symbiotic relationship and process depends on the church and school serving each other, working together to prepare leaders who will lead local churches to advance the fulfillment of the Great Commission. Each party must recognize and affirm the unique contribution that the other makes to this endeavor.

How the Church Can Serve the School

The church needs to affirm the teaching gift as expressed in the training institution. Throughout the Old Testament (OT) and NT, teaching has been prescribed and described as a primary means of perpetuating God's truth in the lives of his people and of introducing it to those who are not in relationship with him (Deut 4:1–14; 6:4–9; 11:18–25; Ezra 7:1–10; Matt

2. Warrington, "Pentecostal Theological Education," 9.

28:16–20; Acts 2:41–42; 18:9–10; 28:30–31; Rom 16:17; 1 Tim 4:11–16; 2 Tim 2:2; 3:10–17). The teaching of Jesus and of the apostolic church was charismatic and transformative. Teaching was understood as a spiritual gift, and teachers were considered gifts to the church, along with other God-called leaders. Unfortunately, the teaching gift has sometimes been routinized and not appreciated as it is described in the NT.[3]

The church must do its part to ensure that schools have qualified educators, and not in just academic terms. Those who train the coming generation of spiritual leaders must responsibly certify those leaders as genuinely Christian in experience and belief.[4]

> New Testament teachers were never mere scholars, seeking truth for truth's sake. They were never mere purveyors of ideas. They were themselves transformed and gifted persons who accepted the Great Commission imperative to teach their charges to obey everything Christ commanded and who were supernaturally aided in the process.[5]

Both Jesus and Paul invested themselves heavily in those who would continue the teaching ministry in their absence. This investment of time, energy, and resources is sometimes not adequately understood or appreciated by the contemporary church.[6]

The church is also responsible to protect its educators and the schools where they teach. Denominational leaders need to safeguard educators against rumors or accusations coming from outside the institution. The institution should also be under the protection of denominational leadership if one of its educators departs from the organization's standards or beliefs and refuses to leave.[7]

How the School Can Serve the Church

The relationship between the school and the church is reciprocal. The school can serve the church by:

3. Lee, "What the Academy Needs," 312–14.
4. Lee, "What the Academy Needs," 314–15.
5. Lee, "What the Academy Needs," 315.
6. Lee, "What the Academy Needs," 315–17.
7. Lee, "What the Academy Needs," 317–18.

1. Using its resources to provide ways of explaining and clarifying the church's theological framework and beliefs;[8]

2. Affirming and encouraging the church's work in every possible way, thus demonstrating its relevance, value, and importance to the church;

3. Providing the needed theological reflection that will be a stabilizing and substantive foundation for the spiritual renewal and encounter that the church experiences;

4. Encouraging evangelism, disciple making, and church planting, and providing the church with new strategies for these endeavors;

5. Being a resource center for the church that will encourage ongoing spiritual renewal in the church.[9]

FOUR INDISPENSABLE AREAS OF PARTNERSHIP

Specific elements can be objectively examined, so educators and church leaders can know the quality and health of the relationship between church and school. When establishing a new training program, these elements must be intentionally set in place. Any existing program can be strengthened by establishing and maintaining these four elements:

1. Student recruitment;

2. Financial support;

3. Church ministry assignments;

4. Cooperation to create and update training process and content based on the priority of equipping the most effective local church leaders.

8. While it is beyond the scope of this book, a study of how the lack of relationship, accountability, and partnership between the church at the local and denominational level in the West during the last few centuries has contributed to the many profound departures from historical theological orthodoxy. We have seen and are continuing to see the fruit of this process on many levels in the last half of the twentieth century and the early decades of the twenty-first century.

9. Dresselhaus, "What Can the Academy Do," 321–22.

Student Recruitment

Recruitment of students is an essential part of the delivery of training.[10] At first glance, this may seem to be just a practical issue. However, it is first a theological issue, because it is connected to the universality of the promise of the outpouring of the Spirit, a core ingredient of Pentecostalism and other renewal movements.[11]

Demographic trends in much of the world, especially in the West and Two-Thirds World, indicate a slowdown in birth rates that leads to a gradual increase in median and average age. Recruitment efforts among the various age, work, and family status demographics should reflect this demographic shift.[12]

Student recruitment for ministerial and local church leadership training should exist as a high priority and as an intentional part of the local church's ministry. This is reflected in the urgency and importance that Jesus placed on this need: "Seeing the people, He felt compassion for them, because they were distressed and dispirited like sheep without a shepherd. Then He said to His disciples, 'The harvest is plentiful, but the workers are few. Therefore beseech the Lord of the harvest to send out workers into His harvest'" (Matt 9:36–38).

Church leaders should recognize those in various demographics who may feel called to ministry and include them in an appropriate ministry track that can prepare them for more formal training.[13] The specifics of that track depend on their age, work and family situation, the particulars of what God has called them to do, and other relevant factors. Their experience in this process will provide them with appropriate preparation for their season of formal study in the institution.

---

10. Recruitment should be seen in much broader terms than just going to churches or youth events and inviting young people to attend Bible school. This strategy can be effective, but it sometimes appears to lack the purposeful, intentional process of cooperation between church and school that provides a way to prepare students who sense a call to ministry and who demonstrate the willingness and ability to prepare for it.

11. Stronstad, *Charismatic Theology*, 25–26, 56–58. See ch. 8 of this book, "Demographic Expansion of Training."

12. See ch. 12 of this book, "The Twenty-First-Century Ecology."

13. Barna Group, *Gen Z*, 88–89. This would potentially help youth pastors in some local churches commonly challenged by finding themselves trying to minister to teens within a wide range of spiritual maturity. Such a ministry track might allow the youth pastor to serve those at a higher level of maturity, while freeing the leader to provide activities more outreach-oriented and/or evangelistic.

Student recruitment events and processes will prove most effective when done as a joint activity between the school and local church. Event-based recruitment such as school representatives speaking at church, youth services and camps, and denominational events, is productive. Annual alumni events and graduation events at schools also have potential for recruitment.

At the same time, other ongoing processes and relationships can supplement these events and deepen the relationship between the school and church. Stakeholders[14] should study those processes and relationships to determine how best to utilize them for this purpose. As the relationship between church and school becomes deeper and healthier, student recruitment should naturally result. Some possible processes like this include joint worker training events throughout the year, cooperative church planting projects or other outreach/missions times during the summer, and annual campus days for potential students and their families to visit and experience life at the school.

The inclusion and participation of all stakeholders (denominational leaders, pastors, interested church members and leaders, school administrators and educators at the school, alumni, and even current students) in the process of recruiting students is key to effective recruitment. These stakeholders can pray and dialogue together to generate new ideas and creative ways to recruit students.

Stakeholders should regard students and potential students as an asset to the school and the church. This reflects the biblical truth that pastors and other spiritual leaders serve as Christ's gift to the church (see Eph 4:7–12). By attributing value to the future pastors and other local church leaders through meeting their needs, these stakeholders will help ensure partnership between the church and school, along with the best possible training for the next generation of leaders.

Financial Support

A second indispensable area of partnership has to do with financial support. Economics may provide the most objective measure of how aware

14. Stakeholders include the various groups with a vested interest in the school, who should have opportunity to provide input into the recruiting process and other items in this section. Stakeholders may include educators, pastors, alumni, and church members with personal interest or professional backgrounds relevant to ministerial training.

the church is of the need for partnership. Edgar Lee encourages the church to take financial responsibility for training institutions and for those who teach there.[15] This is a common concern among denominational leaders and school administrators, and they call for tangible economic support for both students and their ministry training schools.[16]

Ongoing, systematic financial support does not happen without congregations being convinced of the validity of ministerial training. Financial support for schools that is motivated by guilt or compassion for struggling college students does not prove sustainable. The ideal of consistent financial support from the constituency (both churches and individuals or businesses with economic resources)[17] will come rather as the result of several motivators:

1. Educators and leaders must provide potential givers with a theological basis for supporting a ministry training school, thus providing an objective foundation for a conviction about giving;

2. The constituency must feel a sense of ownership and partnership with the institution;

3. The constituency should regularly hear testimonials and observe demonstrations of the school's validity, relevance, and importance;

4. Donors must be given regular opportunities to give in as convenient a way as possible.

Church Ministry Assignments

Tremendous potential exists for churches, schools, and students to partner together through church ministry assignments. These assignments can enrich students' training experience by deepening their spiritual formation and sharpening their relational and ministry skills. Church and school personnel must consult together to determine the most appropriate

15. Lee, "What the Academy Needs," 317.

16. Cipriano G. Mortel, Reynaldo Fernando, and Tomas Dulatas, interview by author, Valenzuela, Phil., Sept. 26, 2018. I have observed that generating consistent church support for schools is challenging.

17. See Tan, "Theological Education in Asia," 84–85. Derek Tan ties the tendency of Christian businesses providing financial support to institutions' involvement in making training opportunities available to the laity as well as those called to full-time ministry.

assignments for students, based on each student's maturity, experience, capabilities, and so on. This will enable emerging spiritual leaders to advance in their development and have a greater impact on future generations.

Related to nurturing Pentecostal distinctives as desired goals of training, Jon Ruthven observes that "the goals, then, for NT discipleship training seem to focus on developing the skills needed to replicate the mission of Jesus. If we are to take the commissions of Jesus seriously, these skills would include prayer, faith (for healings, exorcisms and freedom from sin), and aggressive evangelism and mission."[18] There are many aspects of ministerial training, such as those Ruthven mentions, that reflect biblical and Pentecostal and charismatic values that can take place only outside the traditional classroom setting.

Paul's mentorship of Timothy was intertwined with ministry assignments in the churches Paul founded.[19] Ministry training and ministry work cannot and must not be separated.[20] Schools and their partner churches can increase the effectiveness of training by addressing this aspect of students' experiences. Although creating and maintaining this kind of synergistic relationship is challenging, it will produce long-term results of great benefit to both institutions and to students. Dresselhaus insists:

> It is time for a spirit of trust and reciprocity to so grip both the academy and the church that their work together will both please the Lord and build His kingdom. God-given gifts are needlessly squandered when the church distrusts the academy and the academy fails to rise to the task of serving the church. Imagine the influence created by a solid partnership of mutual trust and service between the academy and the church. Its creation must be priority.[21]

AG ministers in the Philippines were asked to respond to this statement: "When I was studying I was involved in local church ministry, but that experience was not very helpful to my development as a minister."[22] Response to this statement was intended to measure how ministers perceived the effectiveness of local church and training institution cooperation in the training process. Although 47 percent saw their experience as

18. Ruthven, *What's Wrong*, 259–60.

19. Miller, "Proposal," 33–37, 40–41.

20. González, *History of Theological Education*, 125–27.

21. Dresselhaus, "What Can the Academy Do," 322.

22. Miller, "Proposal," 132.

positive, 34 percent felt that theirs was deficient. A positive experience may have resulted more from the work of a conscientious pastor than from an intentional, collaborative relationship between the church and the school.

In the same survey of AG ministers, 95 percent agreed that "experiences outside the classroom, such as chapel and small groups, and ministry or work assignments, helped me to grow spiritually and to develop good ministry skills."[23] In addition to the benefits they bring to the school-church relationship, church ministry assignments (along with other experiences outside the classroom) have remarkable potential for contributing to students' spiritual formation and growth in practical ministry skills.

Cooperation in Updating Training Process and Content

Fourth, partnership between the church (at the local and denominational level) and the training institution must remain a priority. Benjamin Sun also advocates for an intentionally formed symbiotic relationship between the church and training institution. He appeals to both parties to work creatively together for ministry models in general and, by implication, ministerial training:

> The church and theological institution should be partners in exploring new ministry models. The church and theological institution can inform one another of the impact of current cultural trends, issues and needs. Open channels of communications between the two are important. This may take place in an informal discussion session or a within a formal structure such as appointing a pastor's advisory committee to the institution.[24]

This symbiotic relationship can create a synergy and long-term growth dynamic for both church and school. The two can work together in the process of updating curriculum and training strategies. Each entity has resources and perspectives to share with the other about current and anticipated needs in the church culture and general culture. They can work together as partners to sharpen and refine the various aspects of the training process to maintain relevance.

23. Miller, "Proposal," 129.

24. Sun, "Assemblies of God," 244. See also his argument for creatively serving those who for various reasons are unable to receive training at a traditional residential campus, 244–46.

The quality and relevance of the training given to pastors and other local church leaders affects every person, family, and demographic in the churches. Therefore, leaders and educators will find it advantageous to encourage input from as broad a base as possible of informed stakeholders to increase the quality of training.

Denominational leadership can create a group of stakeholders (official or unofficial), made up of themselves, local pastors and church members, school administration and faculty, and others with a vested interest or relevant skills or background. This group could meet regularly for prayer and consultation about training processes and content and report their findings to denominational and school leadership.

NON-FORMAL OR INFORMAL TRAINING

In Pentecostal and other renewal movements, the lack of a pronounced clergy-laity distinction, especially in early generations of Pentecostals, made the training of members as lay ministers a natural part of leadership development.[25] This is especially important to remember because of the historic tendency of renewal movements to trend toward a clergy-laity divide.[26]

Some observers of Pentecostal ministerial training have seen non-formal or informal in-service training as even more effective and efficient than traditional, formal training.[27] Although too much of a distinction can be made between formal and informal or non-formal education,[28] simply maintaining a particular model or style of training must never take precedence over the real goal: developing genuinely Spirit-filled local church leaders.[29] Educators must remain open to ways of improving the educational process and opportunities to access it. Informal and non-formal training opportunities provided by local churches are naturally more accessible to local congregations than a Bible institute and give opportunity to those gifted for congregational leadership beyond evangelism and small groups to move to higher levels of leadership.[30]

25. See Klaus and Triplett, "National Leadership," 226.

26. Warrington, *Pentecostal Theology*, 135.

27. See Klaus and Triplett, "National Leadership," 228–29.

28. Hodkinson et al., "Interrelationships."

29. Hodges, *Indigenous Church*, 65.

30. See Klaus and Triplett, "National Leadership," 228–29. It should be noted that this

Informal learning can be generally understood as interpersonal, unstructured interactions that enculturate people further into the group and its values. Non-formal learning is more planned and focused on practices and is often an in-service type of training. Formal education is of longer duration, is planned, and focuses more on the theoretical.[31]

Some ways to make training available at the local church level include night Bible school classes for those who work full-time or small Bible institutes for members who want to study part-time for ministry. Churches may need to be made more aware of such opportunities and encouraged to try them. A major challenge might involve finding qualified instructors. Educators would need to emphasize the advantages of such a local church-based training platform (lower overhead, schedule flexibility, increased accessibility of training opportunities, and so on).

Utilizing available technologies and other resources to do this is a contemporary expression of the values that have historically driven innovation in AG and other Pentecostal and charismatic ministerial training. These technologies can increase the local church's potential to offer less formal and non-traditional training opportunities:

> More and more there is a demand for alternate delivery channels for teaching and learning. Students do not want to quit what they are doing and to study full-time. They are interested in some form of distance learning. As such Pentecostal education needs to be imparted in new ways. Some of the current ways are online courses, modular sessions, and blended forms of distance learning. Teaching an online course is different from teaching a live session. Aside from the internet challenges, the dynamics of teaching also changes. A teacher may or may not have face to face time with the students to find ways to interact with them. This is also dependent on internet availability and efficiency. Decisions have to be made on how much information to post online, whether or not to have streaming video or audio, and how to administer assignments or exams. Modules are a little closer to the traditional classroom setting except for the time factor. Teachers will have to be able to cover all the material in the time given. Students respond differently when they are pressured in a short time. They do not have much time to process what they are learning. In some cases, there is a need to blend the forms of distance learning. In places where the internet connection is slow, CDs may be prepared for students

---

might include people who do not fit into traditional academic standards.

31. Elliston, *Home Grown Leaders*, 34, 136–37.

to use. Interaction may still be through e-mail if possible. Skype calls may or may not be possible.[32]

CONCLUSION

Although speaking primarily of seminary education, Justo González advocates for seven actions that can help bring ministry training back to a place of relevance and service to the church at the local and denominational level:

1. Establish or re-establish a strong organic relationship between the training institution (students, faculty, and administration) and the local church community;

2. Focus less on the volume of information learned, and more on enabling students to communicate what they have learned to those they serve in effective and transformative ways;

3. Understand and practice theological education as a transformative process that continues throughout the learners' (both leaders and church members) lifetimes;

4. Create the kinds of teaching/learning processes that will enable both congregational leaders and members to wisely and effectively address unexpected moral, ethical, and theological challenges;

5. Open up opportunities for study to more than the traditional demographic wanting ministry training (this includes those who want enrichment and equipping but who do not sense a call to ministry and those already in ministry who want to continue their education);

6. Encourage educators and other spiritual leaders to become mentors, and offer opportunities to learn how to become effective mentors in both the school and local congregation;

7. Produce and affirm curricula that will provide resources for doing these things.[33]

Both the church and the training institution have a vital role in fulfilling God's redemptive purpose in the world. Church members, ordinary disciples, are the chosen means for making other disciples. However, the

---

32. Chai, "Pentecostal Theological Education," 357–58.
33. González, *History of Theological Education*, 127–30.

divine synergy of a Spirit-anointed congregation made up of ordinary disciples and located in a geographical community multiplies the potential of the witness of individuals involved.

In order to further reach its potential, such a congregation needs God-called, Spirit-enabled leadership. Both institutions—church and school—share the privilege and responsibility of selecting and preparing such leaders. As the church and school live out this process by serving one another, God is pleased and glorified. Jesus's prayer in Matt 9:36–38[34] is in the process of being answered.

---

34. Seeing the crowds, he felt compassion for them, because they were distressed and downcast, like sheep without a shepherd. Then he said to his disciples, "The harvest is plentiful, but the workers are few. Therefore, plead with the Lord of the harvest to send out workers into his harvest."

Chapter 3

The Church and Home-Grown Leaders

INTRODUCTION

I WELL REMEMBER THE experience of leaving my hometown and the small AG church I had been a part of for over two years to go off to Bible school in 1976.[1] This kind of thing was a gateway event, ending one era in life and beginning a new one. It was right for churches to celebrate (with a mixture of tears and joy) the departure of young people to begin this new season of discovery and growth. At the same time, at the risk of sounding critical, in retrospect it seems that no one was thinking much about the powerful role the congregation had already played in making that moment possible and about the reality that the aspiring Bible college student was not actually at the beginning point of following God's call on his or her life.

> When Jesus selected His disciples, He had several options available to equip His disciples. The Jews had formal educational means available in the synagogue schools. Paul was formally trained as a Pharisee by Gamaliel. Greek schools were also well known. However, Jesus did not choose schools as the primary model to equip His followers to become leaders. That approach would not be followed until later in the life of the church. He chose rather a nonformal mix of dialogue, experience and reflection.[2]

1. I should actually say *we*. Deborah and I had been married for about fifteen months when we went to Bible college together.

2. Elliston, *Home Grown Leaders*, 48–49.

Implicit throughout this study is the idea of individuals and couples coming up through the ranks of a local congregation, their home church, being trained for ministry there, and ultimately assuming a pastoral leadership role there or elsewhere. The local church has a vital part in preparing people to respond to a call to ministry.[3] This chapter explores various issues related to the local church as an active partner in the training (not just in the preparation for training) of spiritual leaders for congregational leadership. It also advocates for the local church as a source of effective ministry training/formation in its own right.

MINISTRY TRAINING AS AN EXTENSION OF THE DISCIPLESHIP MANDATE

The Great Commission is a mandate to form disciples of Christ through Spirit-empowered proclamation and transformative teaching. This requires the training and equipping of lay people to do charismatic ministry and must be part of the local church's DNA, self-image, and structure. Raising up and training home grown church leaders is not precisely identical to this, but it seems to be a logical extension and implication of it.[4]

The qualifications for spiritual leadership listed in 1 Tim 3:2–7 (primarily observable moral qualities, but also including cognitive knowledge and ministry and relational skills)[5] can be readily recognized in the home church of those who feel called to ministry. Over time, leadership and members in the local congregation can observe someone's progress and consistency in the development of these qualities and skills. In fact, their knowledge of Timothy's life, gained by the ability to observe him over time, enabled the congregation and leaders of his church (and possibly neighboring congregations)[6] to endorse him to travel and work with Paul (Acts 16:1–3). This reality is especially relevant for those unable to access traditional Bible school training because of work or family responsibilities or other reasons. Because formal training institutions should align training content and process with the biblical qualifications for spiritual leaders, the

---

3. See Timothy's experiences in ch. 6 of this book, "The Training Process in Scripture."

4. Elliston, *Home Grown Leaders*, 95–96.

5. See the charts in ch. 5 of this book, "The Development of Spiritual Leaders."

6. In Acts 16:1–3, Luke mentions three cities: Derbe, Lystra, and Iconium. There were no doubt multiple congregations in these cities who may have been familiar with Timothy and his good testimony.

local church is a natural setting for forming people with these qualities and qualifications for spiritual leadership.

THE CHURCH AS A TRAINING CENTER

Ministry formation as described in the Bible most naturally occurs within a ministry context, not in isolation from it.[7] The local church, as the entity on the front lines of advancing God's redemptive purpose in the world and in its immediate community, serves as the most logical setting for this to happen.[8] Separating theoretical, cognitive aspects of training from direct involvement in mission—and compartmentalizing the two aspects of training by creating a wall between them—goes against the biblical model.

The home church of individuals or couples called to ministry, who also have work or family responsibilities, can and should help them. The church can provide nurturing toward leadership and opportunities to be formed for leadership. As non-traditional study opportunities become available, these individuals and couples then would not need to make the choice between formal study and work or family.

CHURCH AND LEADERSHIP MULTIPLICATION

There is a natural, symbiotic bond between church multiplication movements and the rapid, effective development of leaders for the newly planted churches.[9] It is an error to view leadership development and evangelism as two separate categories in the church multiplication movement. Leaders must integrate these aspects (as Jesus demonstrated in training the Twelve) with each other, and they should allow both practices to serve as an integral part of the movement.[10] Both evangelism and leadership development logically take place in the context of the local church.

Ruthven agrees about the natural integration of leadership development and evangelism, asserting that "Christian ministry training occurs

7. Ruthven, *What's Wrong*, 259–63; Banks, *Reenvisioning Theological Education*, 131–33.

8. This is not intended to exclude the many parachurch organizations and ministries that serve alongside the local church to fulfill its purpose in the community.

9. Logan, *Be Fruitful and Multiply*, 33–38.

10. Logan, *Be Fruitful and Multiply*, 34–35.

best within the actual practice of advancing the kingdom of God."[11] In this passage, Ruthven cites Robert Banks's assessment of how apostolic church leaders gathered concentric circles of followers for the specific purpose of involving them actively in mission and ministry. In this involvement, the followers were by default formed into the spiritual leaders that congregations needed.[12]

Formation of a leadership community in the local church provides an effective and biblical way to develop leaders for the local church.[13] Bill Hull's advocacy of this idea is modeled on Paul's method of developing a group of church leaders at Ephesus (Acts 19), and it emulates Jesus's focus on preparing the Twelve for leadership in the church. One notable result of the in-house development of leaders that Hull describes is the formation of additional people called to full-time ministry as pastors, church planters, and missionaries.[14]

LEADERSHIP SELECTION/PREPARATION IN THE LOCAL CHURCH

Edgar Elliston summarizes a number of biblical terms used to describe the selection of leaders. In the OT, the predominant idea is testing under observation. In the NT, a principal idea revolves around a call to move from one place or condition to another.[15] This call comes from God, and although volunteerism is a commendable motivation, it is insufficient. God calls and imparts gifts to enable those called. He forms, equips, and prepares them through the work of existing leaders. The entire process is superintended by the Holy Spirit.[16]

Harold Longenecker describes how the local church can serve as the ideal and most natural setting for preparing people for ministry. A foundational part of this process entails facilitating and recognizing an individual's realization and acquisition of a personal vision. This vision is not the same

---

11. Ruthven, *What's Wrong*, 261–62.

12. Banks, *Reenvisioning Theological Education*, 123.

13. Hull, *Disciple-Making Church*, 191–204.

14. Hull, *Disciple-Making Church*, 198–99.

15. Elliston, *Home Grown Leaders*, 45.

16. Elliston, *Home Grown Leaders*, 45–47.

as multiple, evolving task-related visions. It is essentially the realization by the individual that God can actually use him or her in a significant way.[17]

Each element of this process of selection and preparation should be an intentional part of the local church's program for fulfilling the Great Commission. The local church should by default be aggressively empowering and equipping its own members for ministry in its own community. It should also remain aware of its privilege and responsibility to provide the seedbed (or seminary)[18] for those called as spiritual leaders to shepherd God's saving mission in other areas or settings. The Holy Spirit can use it to prepare them to cross geographic, cultural, ethnic, linguistic, religious, and other boundaries to do so.

THE LOCAL CHURCH AND THE SELECTION/ PREPARATION PROCESS

Existing leaders,[19] under the guidance of the Spirit and with the willing cooperation of emerging leaders, have a singularly essential role in the process of forming those emerging leaders.[20] Elliston sees an analogy between this process and horticulture.[21] Although the process he describes is not identical with the four-phase process, described by Longenecker, that Jesus employed in training the Twelve,[22] the two descriptions fit well conceptually with each other.

Discernment in this process relates to three factors: God's plan and direction in a given situation, the emerging leader(s), and how these factors

---

17. Longenecker, *Growing Leaders by Design*, 119–21. This realization, in whatever way it comes, is part of the call to ministry.

18. González, *History of Theological Education*, 80–81, 114. However, the seminary/ seedbed concept originally sought to keep students from things, people, and circumstances that would distract them from their studies and preparation for priesthood. This view of the seedbed is much different. In it, the local church is grooming—in the midst of mission and all its distractions, interruptions, challenges, and so on—those among its members who might experience a call to full-time ministry.

19. This is true in every setting where spiritual leaders are being formed by educators, denominational leaders, and so on, including the local church. However, this discussion will focus specifically on existing leaders in the local church.

20. Elliston, *Home Grown Leaders*, 109–51.

21. Elliston, *Home Grown Leaders*, 96–98, 109–10.

22. Longenecker, *Growing Leaders by Design*, 39–70.

intersect with each other.[23] Selection of emerging leaders is based on knowledge of and relationship with them. This relational knowledge recognizes their "giftedness, motivations, present level of ability or competence and sense of calling"[24] along with leadership traits[25] that they have and are developing.[26]

This book's main focus is the formation of pastoral leaders for the local church. Depending on denominational polity, there are various levels of influence that a sending local church and its leadership might have on what Elliston describes as the context, initial followers, and initial ministry assignment[27] of emerging leaders. However, exercising these principles while such emerging leaders are coming up through the ranks of their local church remains vital in the process of forming those leaders.

Existing leaders are responsible for the process of empowering emerging leaders. Elliston describes power as existing in various categories (spiritual, social, and positional). One can understand existing leaders as power brokers responsible to share spiritual power, which is expansive and belongs to God, with emerging leaders.[28] Spiritual authority is founded on the leader's growing relationship with God and is the basis for exercising spiritual power. Followers willingly acknowledge these attributes as they see them at work in both existing and emerging leaders.[29]

PARTNERSHIP WITH TRAINING INSTITUTIONS

One must understand that the option of training for a call to ministry at the home church or at a formal training institution need not be an either/or proposition. Individuals and couples called into ministry can continue their involvement with their home church while using technology or other means such as short-term training modules to access more formal

23. Elliston, *Home Grown Leaders*, 110–14.

24. Elliston, *Home Grown Leaders*, 116.

25. A plethora of listings describes such traits and skills. These characteristics include adaptability, situational awareness, dependability, assertiveness and persuasiveness, amenability, persistence and self-confidence, ability to communicate effectively, diplomacy and tact, along with task orientation and a sense of responsibility and accountability.

26. Elliston, *Home Grown Leaders*, 114–17.

27. Elliston, *Home Grown Leaders*, 117–24.

28. Elliston, *Home Grown Leaders*, 124–30.

29. Elliston, *Home Grown Leaders*, 131–36.

opportunities for academic training. Training opportunities at the denominational level may also exist, serving people who cannot or who choose not to use more traditional platforms of ministry training.

It is in the best interest of training institutions to see themselves as partners at both the local and denominational level with churches that desire to intentionally raise up home grown leaders, rather than see such ministries as competition. This kind of partnership can work as a type of apprenticeship,[30] where those called to ministry can experience formation in mission rather than for mission.[31] Such a partnership can utilize digital technology, extension campuses, and so on in the training process to meet the need for more formal aspects of training.

One concern of many potential students and their families is the cost of attending traditional training institutions. Some may feel it inappropriate to compare the relative expense of institutional and local church ministry training. The idea that no price can be put on the value of such study does not cancel out the biblical and practical necessity of thrift and the prudent use of economic resources. In reality, pastors, denominational leaders, and educators know that formal education is becoming more expensive all the time.[32] A quick survey of Christian university websites reveals the massive economic investment required to receive a ministry degree. This expense raises enormous concerns among institutions.[33] In light of this, the economic advantage of the process of developing home grown leadership is obvious.

CONCLUSION

Both Jesus and Paul appear to intentionally have built their leadership development strategy around the practice of placing their protégés squarely in the middle of ministry situations. They also built into the training process the means to increase cognitive knowledge, ministry and relational skills, and spiritual formation simultaneously. While it may certainly be useful to catalogue each of these categories of ministry formation separately for the purpose of understanding each one better, it does not follow that they should be artificially compartmentalized in the training process itself. The

30. Portmann, "Intentional Apprenticing," 16–28.

31. Banks, *Reenvisioning Theological Education,* 135–36.

32. González, *History of Theological Education,* x.

33. Association of Theological Schools, "Resources to Address Cost."

local church provides the ideal place for this kind of holistic process to take place. The conditions for this to happen are simple but challenging. First, the church leadership must make the connection theologically and see the potential for the advancement of God's kingdom. Second, they must be willing to commit themselves and whatever resources are needed to accomplish it. Third, they must be willing to give away the results of their investment in the lives of those whom God has called to full-time ministry.

Unit 2: Spiritual Leadership

Chapter 4

The Spirit in the World and in the Church

INTRODUCTION

THE FOCUS OF THIS chapter is not pneumatology *per se*, although its content rests on a biblical understanding of the work of the Spirit.[1] Instead, the focus is the work of the Spirit in both the world and the church, and how that dynamic interaction should influence the content and process of ministerial training in the twenty-first century. The work of the Spirit is to enable, guide, and empower the local church and its members to advance God's redemptive purpose through fulfilling the Great Commission in the community where it exists.[2] That purpose is fulfilled through the church's anointed witness for Christ (proclamation), its transformative teaching (making disciples), and its incorporation of believers into its fellowship to be prepared and empowered to continue the mission.

This chapter will begin by briefly answering three questions:

1. How does the Spirit prepare and enable the local congregation to carry out the Great Commission?

---

1. For a survey of the work of the Spirit in Scripture, see Horton, *What the Bible Says.* For a more systematic treatment of pneumatology, see McLean, "Holy Spirit."

2. Although there is a great deal of discussion about the virtual church and its potential to reach beyond its physical proximity, that topic is beyond the scope of this chapter. For information on this topic, see Estes, *Simchurch*; see also Dyer, *From Garden to City.*

2. How does the Spirit work in the lives of the people (individuals, families, neighborhoods) in proximity to the church to draw them to Christ, disciple them, and incorporate them into the congregation?

3. How does the Spirit work in and through the leaders of the local church to oversee/shepherd the process?

The chapter then suggests implications from the answers about how to best prepare Spirit-filled leaders for local churches who can most effectively lead their congregations in the fulfillment of the Great Commission in their communities.

THE SPIRIT PREPARES AND ENABLES THE CONGREGATION

Regardless of when the NT church was constituted and inaugurated, the day of Pentecost in Acts 2 and the Johannine Pentecost in John 20:19–23 are foundational to its being. At its core, Christ's church is pneumatic and charismatic: "By its very nature as the body of Christ, the Church is integrally dependent on the finished work of Christ on earth (his death, resurrection, and ascension) and the coming of the Holy Spirit (John 16:7; Acts 20:28; 1 Cor. 12:13)."[3]

The Spirit is also intimately involved with the church in the process of edifying and building it up so that it can mature and serve the needs of its members. In Eph 4:16, the same Spirit who unifies the believers in one body (vv. 3–4) directs the process aimed at the building up (*oikodome*) of the body in love until it reaches maturity in Christ. There does not seem to be any overt reference to the more charismatic activity of the Spirit as the process is described here.

In 1 Cor 14:12 and 26, the same building up and edifying terminology from Eph 4 (*oikodome*) that is to benefit the congregation is used. In this case, the context is clearly the more dynamic, vocal manifestations of the Spirit. The church is edified as it experiences and responds to charismatic utterances and other more spontaneous workings of the Spirit.

One point in both of these passages is that the Spirit is faithfully at work, whether his gifts are manifested in more extraordinary ways or in ways that seem mundane. The underlying purpose of both kinds of manifestation is the same: to strengthen and impart health to the congregation.

3. See Dusing, "New Testament Church," 528–29.

As this takes place, both individual believers and the corporate body experience increasing Christlikeness as they mature and gain increasing stability in their faith. They are then able to communicate the message of Christ effectively, with authority and with the supernatural enablement of the Spirit.

The desired result of this process is proclamation of the gospel that leads to faith and repentance, as well as transformative teaching that produces an expanding group of maturing disciples. This process is the outcome of a partnership or interaction between believers and the Spirit.[4] God's mission, understood in this way, is the church's reason for being and is a major focus of the Spirit's work in the world. Without this purpose, the church has no overarching and definitive purpose in the world.[5]

THE SPIRIT'S WORK IN THE LIVES OF COMMUNITY MEMBERS

Biblical-Theological Foundation

While the Holy Spirit is engaged with the congregation individually and corporately and is actively involved in those processes of growth, that is not the only setting in which he is working. He is also involved, usually quietly, in the lives of those outside the congregation and outside the faith. He has done this throughout history.[6] The Spirit is "the active agent of the Godhead in His dealings with the creation."[7] This section will look briefly at the ways in which he is at work to prepare people to hear the gospel through the witness of the local church.

One of many great contributions of John Wesley to theology is what Wesley called prevenient grace. This is in contrast to what Calvin called common grace.[8] In Wesley's view, prevenient grace is the first of three ways in which humans experience God's grace. The second is justifying grace, experienced as an individual repents of sin and places his or her faith in

4. See Dusing, "New Testament Church," 544; See Klaus, "Mission of the Church," 572–75.

5. See Klaus, "Mission of the Church," 572–75; Alvarez, "Distinctives of Pentecostal Education," 286.

6. See McLean, "Holy Spirit," 392–93.

7. See McLean, "Holy Spirit," 377.

8. Dragos, "What Is Prevenient Grace?"

Christ, bringing the individual to regeneration and salvation. The third is sanctifying grace, a process that begins at salvation and carries the new believer toward maturity and completion in Christ. The four primary passages Wesley saw as foundational to understanding prevenient grace are John 1:9; 12:32; Rom 2:4; and Titus 2:11.[9]

Although the term prevenient grace is not used in Scripture, it can be discerned in the process of how God the Holy Spirit works in the lives of those described in Scripture. While it is not universalist in the sense of guaranteeing salvation ultimately to all, it does offer people the ability to respond positively to the message of the gospel.

The most succinct passage that addresses the Spirit's work in relation to the unbelieving world[10] through prevenient grace may be John 16:7–11. In John 14–16, Jesus discusses what the Spirit's relationship with the disciples will be like in his absence and contrasts their experience of the Spirit with the unbelieving world's lack of ability to perceive Jesus and the Spirit (14:16–17, 19). The world's relationship with the disciples is adversarial, as it was with Jesus (15:18–19), but the Spirit will come to testify—and to enable the disciples to testify—of Jesus (15:26–27).

While we may understand the Spirit's testifying as taking place primarily through the disciples' witness, it should not be understood as taking place exclusively through their direct witness. The Spirit desires to speak and work through the Church individually and corporately, but he is not limited to those options.[11] In fact, it is important to understand the distinctions that exist between the Spirit and the church. The Spirit is free as a member of the Godhead, and the church is made up of sinful people. The Spirit precedes and enlivens the church. The Spirit is also at work in the places, times, and ways in which he in his sovereignty chooses.[12] In light of

---

9. Shelton, "Biblical Case for Prevenient Grace." "There was the true Light which, coming into the world, enlightens every man" (John 1:9). "And I, if I am lifted up from the earth, will draw all men to myself" (John 12:32). "Or do you think lightly of the riches of his kindness and tolerance and patience, not knowing that the kindness of God leads you to repentance?" (Rom 2:4). "For the grace of God has appeared, bringing salvation to all men" (Titus 2:11).

10. Kostenberger, *Theology of John's Gospel*, 281–82. Kostenberger points out that John uses the term κόσμος in three different ways: the physical creation, humanity in general, and, specifically, the sinful and unbelieving humanity.

11. The work of the Spirit in non-Christian religions is beyond the scope of this chapter.

12. Kung, *Church*, 229–36.

this, it should not be surprising when the Spirit chooses to act beyond the perimeters of the local congregation.

This facet of the Spirit's working separately or externally from the church is mentioned numerous times in Luke-Acts.[13] First, the Spirit moves upon people who are under the old covenant (John the Baptist in his mother's womb, Mary, Elizabeth, Anna, and Simeon) to communicate to or through them about the coming of the Messiah.[14] Second, in Acts 4:24–25, the praying church cites Ps 146:6, which refers to God's sovereignty over all creation. The Spirit's striving with backslidden Israel in the OT is a precedent for his striving with any people who need to come to faith and repentance.[15] These workings of the Spirit can occur independently of the presence or existence of a congregation.

The remarkable turn of events that led Peter to speak to the household of Cornelius was orchestrated by the Spirit, independent of the plan or intention of the church and its leaders.[16] The process was so unusual and outside the expectation of Peter and the other leaders that it created a controversy about interaction with and ministry to the Gentiles that was not easily or quickly resolved.

Two similar outside-the-congregation conversions recorded in Acts are the conversion of the Ethiopian eunuch (Acts 8:26–38; with the assistance of Philip) and the conversion of Saul of Tarsus (9:3–9). The strategic importance of the conversion of Saul to the spread of Christianity in Asia Minor and Europe is clear. While it is unclear if the Ethiopian eunuch was instrumental in the spread of Christianity in that part of Africa, it is clear that Luke felt it necessary to record this event. In some situations, it may be necessary for the Spirit to work independently of the church, simply because the ultimate results or even the strategy of working toward those results is beyond what the church or its leadership would have envisioned or found acceptable.

Contemporary Setting

To realize that the Holy Spirit is at work outside the boundary of the congregation and to be committed to working cooperatively with that dynamic

13. Gallagher, "Holy Spirit in the World," 17–33.

14. Gallagher, "Holy Spirit in the World," 23.

15. Gallagher, "Holy Spirit in the World," 23.

16. Gallagher, "Holy Spirit in the World," 31.

process has tremendous potential for application in the local church. The macro situation in a regional or national context has implications for the local setting. Conditions specific to the micro setting will also indicate what the local congregation can or should do to advance God's mission in its community. Leaders of the congregation must remain sensitive to those conditions, how those conditions are evolving, and to how the Spirit may direct them to lead the congregation to serve in a way appropriate to the current or developing conditions.

How do local church leaders see their surrounding community? Leaders must continually ask these questions about the local community they serve:

1. What is the Spirit doing in the lives of individuals, families or households, neighborhoods, and the greater community?

2. What are the demographic characteristics of the surrounding community? Are they changing?

3. What are the religious and other characteristics of the community? Are they changing?

4. What current events are happening, or what past events or processes have shaped the community?

5. What are the current economic conditions of the community? Is there an anticipated change in those conditions?

6. What are the current or potential needs (economic, social, spiritual, emotional, practical) in the community?

7. What entities in the community (schools, government, businesses/ private sector, law enforcement/corrections, social services) seem to be open to the congregation's help or partnership?

To answer some of these questions, leaders must have access to available objective information. To answer other questions, they must cultivate sensitivity to what the Spirit may be saying to them, orchestrating, or allowing in the community. They must also remain relationally (not just physically) present in the community, building rapport with members of all socioeconomic levels and demographic groups.

THE SPIRIT WORKS IN AND THROUGH LOCAL CHURCH LEADERS

Based on the above perspectives about the work of the Spirit in the church and the community where the church exists, what kinds of local church leaders are needed to lead their congregations? I contend that ministerial training should focus on forming the specific qualities and skills that will enable local church leaders to work in tandem with the Holy Spirit as he works in the congregation and the surrounding community.[17] Those qualities and skills will enable them to do two things:

1. Facilitate and cooperate with what Scripture says that the Spirit wants to do in the church;

2. Discern how the church can cooperate with how the Spirit is working in the surrounding community.

What will these leaders look like? While allowing for variety in personality, gifting, calling, passion, etc. that God places in the lives of pastors and other local church leaders, training content and structure should aim at developing the following kinds of characteristics in leaders:

1. A lifestyle that demonstrates ongoing growth in the characteristics listed in 1 Tim 3:2–7;

2. A balance between inward and outward orientation for the life of the church;[18]

3. The ability to see church structure as a means to an end, not an end in itself (structure is a servant, not a master);[19]

4. Understanding and embracing the responsibility of discipling believers, including providing consistent opportunities for encountering the Spirit and equipping/mobilizing them for service;

5. Understanding the times in which we currently live and how the Spirit has worked in the past, with the ability to conceptualize and see the principles at play in past revivals, not just stories of what happened then;

17. Ward, "Servants, Leaders, and Tyrants," 27–42.

18. Lim, *Spiritual Gifts*, 69–70.

19. Koeshall and Koeshall, "Ecclesiology to Go," 14–21; Lim, *Drama of Redemption*, 81–84; see ch. 1 of this book, "The Church and the Holy Spirit."

6. The ability to recognize ways the Spirit is working in the community where the church is located.

IMPLICATIONS FOR TRAINING PROCESS AND CONTENT

We have now arrived at the real point of this chapter. If local churches are to work in tandem with the Holy Spirit in carrying out God's redemptive mission in their communities, they must have leaders who have been formed and trained with this specific goal in mind.[20] If the process and content of training does not reflect this priority, it is doubtful that a large percentage of graduates will ultimately lead their congregations with a sensitivity to what the Spirit is currently doing and ultimately desires to bring about through the church.

I am not attempting to describe what the entirety of a training program should look like. These observations simply suggest elements that should be woven into the process and content of the training and applied with sensitivity to conditions in the area served by the training institution.

Relationship with the Unbelieving Community

I have elsewhere discussed how requirements for spiritual leadership in 1 Tim 3:2–7 seem to emphasize observable character traits over practical skills or task-oriented abilities.[21] While practical skills and abilities remain essential for leading a congregation, Paul gives a reason for the priority of observable character traits. The spiritual leader "must have a good reputation with those outside [the church], so that he will not fall into reproach and the snare of the devil" (v. 7).[22] Facilitating the formation of this kind of life should be a major focus of training, especially in the mentoring process.

---

20. See Rowen, "Missiology," 93–100.

21. See ch. 5 of this book, "The Development of Spiritual Leaders."

22. While "the church" is not in the original, it seems reasonable that it should be inserted to clarify that the spiritual leader must be believable to those in the community beyond the congregation. This will provide moral authority and credibility for his or her and the church's witness.

Personal Involvement with the Community

In addition to students' church ministry assignments, students must, if possible, be personally involved in the community that is in proximity to their assigned church. This is to facilitate a learning experience with a more comprehensive reach than just what ministry they do within the congregation. If this is not feasible, there should be some other significant engagement with a community or neighborhood outside the school.

Community Focus

Students must be taught to orient their ministry—and their attitude toward ministry—as one of pastoring a community, not just a congregation. What they do to minister to the congregation is ultimately to enable it to carry out God's mission in the surrounding community. Outreach focus can only be fulfilled through a healthy congregation.

Missional Ecclesiology

Ecclesiology must be taught as more than denominational history and polity, important as those things are. It must also include instruction on the missional relevance of church government and how church structure is meant to facilitate the equipping and mobilization of the congregation to fulfill its God-given purpose. Structure (organization, scheduling, ministry formats, events, etc.) should never be allowed to inhibit the church's ministry to the community around it. Instead, it should empower and enable the church to more effectively and appropriately serve its community in a redemptive way.

Holistic Team Ministry

Most students may feel passionate about a particular area of ministry (preaching and teaching, evangelism, worship, children, youth, etc.) and understand themselves to be called and gifted for it. They must learn to see their specific, individual ministry as part of an overall holistic ministry balanced between the priorities of God's mission. Ultimately, the church is to be matured so it can increase its potential to reach more people and expanding demographics. Trainers must emphasize each priority without neglecting the other.

Revival/Renewal Theology

Students must be taught more in their study of past revivals than just the events and personalities involved. While this is important and useful information, it is insufficient to help students form a vision for what the Lord may want to do through their lives and ministries. Future local church leaders need to form a theology of revival that can be carried into the contemporary scene. This theology of renewal will provide them with an understanding of revival that can encourage ongoing encounters with the Spirit and at the same time protect them and their congregation from negative tendencies that can damage or destroy the positive effects it is intended to bring. A theology of renewal will also enable students to provide pastoral leadership for revival times that can bring out the healthiest and most enduring fruit possible from the experience.

CONCLUSION

The two most important questions educators must answer are: 1) What kind of spiritual leaders do we want to graduate from this program? 2) What kind of training do we want to offer to those who believe God is calling them to ministry?

Answers to these questions should rest on what we can learn from Scripture about the necessary process, content, and results of the training of spiritual leaders. As when Jesus began his process of training the Twelve, trainers should already have in mind the same desired end result of training.[23] Additionally, the answer to these questions will neither be found in secular models of professional education[24] nor necessarily in ministerial training programs used in the past.[25]

Scripture informs us that the Spirit is at work in the congregation and in the community where that congregation is located. Local church leaders

23. Longenecker, *Growing Leaders by Design*, 31–32.

24. See González, *History of Theological Education*, 43–53; Ruthven, *What's Wrong*, 243–68.

25. See Klaus and Triplett, "National Leadership," 233–34.

must stay attuned to the work of the Spirit in both settings and pay attention to what the Spirit is actually doing—or preparing to do—toward fulfilling God's mission in their world. Thus, ministerial training must prepare leaders to fulfill that function.

Chapter 5

The Development of Spiritual Leaders

INTRODUCTION

HOW SHOULD A TRAINING institution determine content, teaching modalities, and desired outcomes? Many factors affect and influence these decisions. Various organizations, both governmental and non-governmental, have requirements for different kinds and levels of accreditation.[1] Cultural expectations about what constitutes quality secondary education can also affect how spiritual leaders are trained.

While there is nothing inherently wrong with accreditation and cultural ideas about education,[2] in this chapter, I challenge educators to re-examine ministerial training in light of the apostle Paul's requirements for leaders in local churches. These requirements give denominational leaders and educators a window into what desired outcomes should be and thus a means for measuring the value and potential for the proposed content and processes to use in training.

REQUIREMENTS FOR CONGREGATIONAL LEADERS

As a listing of qualifications for leaders in a local congregation, 1 Tim 3:1–7 and Titus 1:5–9 can be viewed as a description of the desired outcomes of

---

1. Banks, *Reenvisioning Theological Education*, 6.
2. Banks, *Reenvisioning Theological Education*, 194–95, 250.

a ministerial training program.[3] This section overviews these passages to discover priorities and deduces what educators should focus on for a regimen of training Spirit-filled leaders for the local congregation.

Charismatic gifting for ministry and leadership in these passages is assumed and not ignored in this description of qualifications for local church leadership.[4] Each passage also addresses local conditions and the needs that Timothy and Titus faced. Timothy's work was with the church (congregations) in Ephesus, which had been a major focus of Paul's ministry (Acts 19). Paul listed for Timothy the qualifications both for bishops to lead and deacons[5] to serve established congregations. He directed Titus to complete the work of establishing and organizing congregations on Crete and limited his list of leadership qualifications to elders.

A bishop (1 Tim 3:1–2; Titus 1:7) would actively and conscientiously oversee the congregation and also provide protection for it.[6] Presbyters[7] or elders (Titus 1:5) may be interchangeable with bishop in this context (note the use of bishop in v. 7).[8] If elder is a correct rendering in Titus 1:5, it cannot refer exclusively to chronological age, because people are either older or not older regardless of being officially appointed as an elder. It seems reasonable to understand eldership primarily as having proven maturity in the faith.[9]

The structure of 1 Tim 3:1–7 is notable and may indicate that much of a potential leader's qualifications revolve around an earned, actual reputation:

3. This is not meant to disregard many other passages that describe requirements for leaders, but rather to emphasize the need to take cues from two concise scriptural descriptions of leadership qualifications and to apply them to the desired aims or results of ministerial training.

4. Jamieson et al., *Commentary*, 2:410; see ch. 4 of this book, "The Spirit in the World and in the Church."

5. I will not address 1 Tim 3:8–13 on qualifications of deacons. It is sufficient to say for the purposes of this chapter that the qualifications for deacons (v. 8, *osautos*, in the same way) may indicate similarity of concept or thought. http://nltinterlinear.com/greekconc/w_9sau_1twv.

6. See Beyer, "Episkopos," 244–48.

7. See Bornkamm, "Presbyteros," 931–35.

8. Willmington, *Bible Handbook*, 734–35.

9. However, "The meaning of the injunction is, that Titus should appoint, out of the number of elderly men of approved Christian reputation, certain ones to be overseers (ἐπίσκοποι) of the churches in the several cities" (Vincent, *Word Studies*, 4:333).

The office of overseer was open to all, but some qualifications needed to be observed, especially in view of the heresy in Ephesus. The qualification of being "above reproach" frames the other qualifications (3:2, 7); this was an ancient way of emphasizing that the qualifications focused on this issue. Political leaders were also expected to be "above reproach," but a persecuted minority sect needed to protect itself against public slander even more than politicians did.[10]

The requirement of being above reproach (1 Tim 3:2, 7; Titus 1:6–7) appears to frame the overall list of qualifications for leadership. In 1 Tim 3, "The need for blamelessness is repeated from verse 6. The reason this quality is so important is that an overseer serves as a steward of God. Damage to a church leader's reputation is damage to God's reputation."[11] In Titus, the requirement to be above reproach precedes both the section on home and family life and the one on personal and ministry life.

While there are differences in the two lists,[12] they are overall very similar conceptually and have notable areas of overlap with each other. The first overlap is the requirement of a life that is above reproach or blameless (1 Tim 3:2, *anepilemptos*; Titus 1:6, *anegkletos*; Titus 1:7, *anegkleton*) and spoken well of (1 Tim 3:7, *martyrian*). This good testimony to those outside the congregation is especially important to Paul.

Another noticeable overlap is the connection of a lifestyle that is characterized by drinking and aggression (1 Tim 3:3; Titus 1:7). This kind of lifestyle is in contrast to being gentle, peaceable, and free from greed in 1 Timothy. It is contrasted to being hospitable, loving what is good, and being sensible, just, devout, and self-controlled in Titus.[13]

An important and interesting overlap is that of teaching. The phrase in 1 Tim 3:2 (*didaktikon*, able to teach) is short and concise, while in Titus 1:9, Paul goes into much more detail: "holding fast the faithful word which is in accordance with the teaching, so that he will be able both to exhort in sound doctrine and to refute those who contradict." The following verses

---

10. Keener, "1 Tim 3:2–3" in *IVP Bible Background Commentary*.

11. See Litfin, "Titus."

12. The most notable is that, unlike 1 Tim 3:6, there is no explicit requirement in Titus that an elder not be a new convert. However, it would be difficult for a new convert to fulfill the qualifications in Titus.

13. In Titus, the negatives of addiction to wine and pugnaciousness are part of a list of five negatives: not being self-willed, quick-tempered, addicted to wine, pugnacious, or fond of sordid gain.

(vv. 10–16), in describing those among the Jewish and Cretan populations who opposed Paul's teaching, seem to clarify why he went into more detail. The elders to be appointed by Titus would face a great deal of pressure and pushback and therefore would need to maintain right teaching among the faithful and to effectively confront wrong teaching among opposers.

Following is a side-by-side listing of the requirements in 1 Tim 3 and Titus 1. While some of these qualities are difficult to categorize, they can be classified in general terms. Each requirement has at least one letter beside it. The letters represent a level of knowledge (K), a skill (S), an observable character trait (C), or a relational trait (R):

1 Tim 3		Titus 1	
Above reproach	C	Above reproach	C
Husband of one wife	C	Husband of one wife	C
Temperate	C	Children who believe, not accused of dissipation or rebellion	K, S, R
Prudent	C	Above reproach	C
Respectable	C	Not self-willed	C
Hospitable	C, S, R	Not quick-tempered	C
Able to teach	K, S	Not addicted to wine	C
Not addicted to wine	C	Not pugnacious	C, R
Not pugnacious	C, R	Not fond of sordid gain	C
Gentle	C, R	Hospitable	C, S, R
Peaceable	C, R	Loves what is good	C
Free from love of money	C	Sensible	C
Manages his own household well	K, S, R	Just	C
Keeps children under control with dignity	S, R	Devout	C
Not a new convert	C	Self-controlled	C
Good reputation with outsiders	C	Holding fast the faithful word	K, S
		Able to exhort in sound doctrine and refute those who contradict	K, S, R

Table 1. Requirements of a Spiritual Leader (1 Tim 3 and Titus 1)

From these listings of qualifications, a continuum of priorities emerges. By far the highest is observable character traits; a distant second is relational traits. Following are skills and knowledge.[14] My contention here is that the priorities and goals of training for leadership of the local church should reflect how these qualifications, taken from 1 Tim 3 and Titus 1, are weighted.

Quality	1 Tim 3	Titus 1	Total
C—Character Trait	13	14	27
R—Relational Trait	6	4	10
S—Skill	4	4	8
K—Knowledge	2	3	5

Table 2. Priorities of Spiritual Leader Requirements

Seeing the essence of the local church as a living, spiritual, organism rather than an inanimate organization, Lawrence Richards and Gib Martin describe the kind of leadership the local church requires.[15] Rather than controlling others' behavior, leaders serve by influencing others through their instruction and example to grow more into the image of Christ.[16] Authority is self-authenticating, so the "leader is followed because his or her character bears the visible stamp of the work of God."[17] Leaders have credibility, not just because of giftedness (or knowledge or developed skills), but because of an observable growth in spiritual maturity.[18]

---

14. As I have stated elsewhere, the prioritizing of observable character traits does not minimize the importance of other qualifications. It does clarify that character is an extremely important area of qualification and may be the most easily overlooked in training. Additionally, differences in the quantity of characteristics should not in itself indicate priority. However, the overall sense of these passages seems to confirm the emphasis I am advocating.

15. L. Richards and Martin, *Theology of Personal Ministry*, 295–302.

16. L. Richards and Martin, *Theology of Personal Ministry*, 296–98.

17. L. Richards and Martin, *Theology of Personal Ministry*, 300.

18. L. Richards and Martin, *Theology of Personal Ministry*, 301–2; See Ward, "With an Eye," 35–36.

FORMATION OF LEADERS

Overview

It is an error to strictly compartmentalize the various areas where spiritual leaders are to be developed—spiritual, practical, relational, and cognitive. All of these need to be sharpened and developed simultaneously, in an integrated, holistic, and nonlinear way.[19] However, it is also helpful to see the particular nature of each area of the person. This helps to understand and address each one.

J. Robert Clinton describes the development and formation of a leader as a lifetime process that can be understood as taking place in six phases.[20] He understands that the lives of biblical leaders and spiritual leaders throughout church history should be studied and used to determine God's process of forming current and emerging leaders. His approach is based on Heb 13:7–8: "Remember those who led you, who spoke the word of God to you; and considering the result of their conduct, imitate their faith. Jesus Christ is the same yesterday and today and forever."[21] The first three phases he describes in the life of a leader are pertinent to this chapter. In general terms, these phases take place while the prospective student is being prepared to recognize God's call to ministry and during the season of (formal) training and early ministry. These phases are Sovereign Foundations, Inner Life Growth, and Ministry Maturing.

In Phase 1, Sovereign Foundations, God works providentially in the unfolding life of the person he has called to spiritual leadership.[22] This is true regardless of the specifics of those events and processes and whether those specifics appear to be positive or negative. Often, especially when they are negative, it is only in retrospect that God's direction (or allowance of those negatives)[23] to bring about his ultimate plan for the leader can be discerned.

---

19. Banks, *Reenvisioning Theological Education*, 123–24.

20. F. Clinton, *Making of a Leader*, 30. These phases are processes that blend and overlap with each other.

21. F. Clinton, *Making of a Leader*, 39.

22. F. Clinton, *Making of a Leader*, 44.

23. It is beyond the scope of this chapter to discuss the theological and philosophical aspects of this challenging subject. My emphasis is that even when negatives happen, God has the ability to bring about his redemptive plan through them or in spite of them.

Henry Blackaby and Richard Blackaby describe the early lives of a number of well-known leaders, both secular and Christian.[24] Contrary to what might be expected, many of those leaders overcame remarkable challenges of many kinds. While the ideal for a child is a home and family life characterized by nurture and encouragement, the absence of these things does not prevent or disqualify God-called leaders from following and fulfilling their call. The same is true for a troubled youth or adulthood.

Clinton calls Phase 2 Inner Life Growth.[25] Here, emerging leaders grow in their relationship with God and undergo various tests (word, obedience, and integrity)[26] intended to facilitate growth in character or to affirm character development that has already occurred, and to sharpen ministry skills and gifting. Potential for leadership may also begin to come to the surface during this phase.

This change in focus from receiving ministry to giving ministry[27] moves the potential leader into Phase 3, Ministry Maturing.[28] During this phase, the emerging leader gives a clear, positive response to the sense of God's call to ministry by accepting a ministry challenge and one or more specific ministry task (entry). This normally takes place in the context of the local church or an outside or parachurch ministry. He or she also begins to develop the practical skills and spiritual giftings needed for effective ministry (training). Training can consist of informal apprenticeships, non-formal workshops, and formal training and is usually a combination of these.[29]

Phase 3 takes place over an extended period of time, including the formal training period and continuing into ministry, following the completion of formal training.[30] While the issues Clinton addresses in the following chapter[31] are experienced primarily when a leader has formally entered into ministry, some may arise during the season of formal training. Similar

---

24. See Blackaby and Blackaby, *Spiritual Leadership*, 52–66.

25. F. Clinton, *Making of a Leader*, 45, 73–74.

26. F. Clinton, *Making of a Leader*, 73.

27. F. Clinton, *Making of a Leader*, 78–79.

28. F. Clinton, *Making of a Leader*, 77–97.

29. F. Clinton, *Making of a Leader*, 90–92.

30. My formal training has been spread over various periods of my life, beginning in 1976 and concluding in 2020.

31. F. Clinton, *Making of a Leader*, 99–124.

to the experiences of the Twelve during their relating phase of training,[32] students may begin to learn important lessons about relating with others in healthy ways. These lessons revolve around authority, relationships, and conflict.[33] Clinton observes that "the authority problem concerns how a leader gets along with people: his leaders, his peers, his subordinates. Influence depends on relationships with people, so many of the lessons learned during this phase will focus on relationships."[34]

The distinctive throughout the entire process of the leader's spiritual formation is that such formation is ultimately God's work.[35] He gives the Holy Spirit, develops the capabilities in leaders, continually forms them through a lifelong process, and calls them to their specific assignments. The season of training is a formative time that the Spirit uses to develop emerging leaders. This season is not an endpoint for growth and transformation; it should be a foundational season that results in spiritual leaders continually responding to the Spirit's direction for personal growth and transformation and facilitating the same kind of new covenant discipleship among those they lead.[36]

Spiritual and Relational

While there are individualized aspects of spiritual formation such as the disciplines of personal prayer and Bible study,[37] it is nearly impossible to divorce spiritual and relational formation from each other. In addition to mentoring,[38] genuine Christian fellowship or *koinonia* must exist as a part of students' training experience. This kind of genuine relating produces higher levels of emotional strength.[39] Making fellowship, self-disclosure, and accountable relationships[40] a part of the training experience yields at least three benefits. First, it creates a greater potential for students' spiritual and relational growth to take place. Second, it provides them with a

32. Longenecker, *Growing Leaders by Design*, 56–62.

33. F. Clinton, *Making of a Leader*, 101–8.

34. F. Clinton, *Making of a Leader*, 105.

35. Blackaby and Blackaby, *Spiritual Leadership*, 67–74.

36. Ruthven, *What's Wrong*, 174–75.

37. Lawrenz, *Dynamics of Spiritual Formation*, 99–100.

38. See ch. 10 in this book, "Mentoring."

39. Portmann, "Intentional Apprenticing," 25–26.

40. Lawrenz, *Dynamics of Spiritual Formation*, 102–7.

practical means to facilitate the same kind of formation for the members of the congregation(s) they will serve after their formal training is completed. Third, over a three- or four-year training program, it provides the actual opportunity for students to learn how to lead these groups effectively and to train others to lead them.[41]

Cognitive

Lawrence Richards sees the training institution as having an unspoken hidden curriculum that conditions its graduates to do local church ministry in the same way that their training was done.[42] While speaking primarily of seminaries, his observations apply to any ministerial training institution. Examples of the forms that this hidden curriculum takes include overemphasis on purely cognitive learning, where knowing information is equated with learning; impersonal one-way communication in the classroom that prevents relational interaction; and individualistic and competitive rather than cooperative ways of motivating students to learn.[43]

Richards suggests more beneficial ways of preparing students for the real world of ministry and for having a more biblical mode of ministry:

1. Personalize learning spaces by having some subjects conducted outside a traditional classroom setting and facilitating more personal interaction between students and instructors;

2. Give more recognition to progress in personal growth and application of learning that is expressed through ministry to others;

3. Encourage and facilitate learning teams among students for some subjects. This can provide them with opportunities to experience the same kind of dynamics that should happen in a local congregation as its members grow together.[44]

---

41. Lawrenz, *Dynamics of Spiritual Formation,* 107–12.

42. L. O. Richards, *Theology of Christian Education,* 158–64; see also Ward, "Servants, Leaders, Tyrants," 27–42. This hidden curriculum is not the same as the one discussed in ch. 7 of this book, "The Spirit in the Training Process."

43. L. O. Richards, *Theology of Christian Education,* 159–60.

44. L. O. Richards, *Theology of Christian Education,* 160–61.

Practical

In critiquing the state of Pentecostal training institutions, Ruthven warns against departing from biblical ways of knowing truth, desired outcomes of training, and instructional methodology.[45] The goals of traditional theological education (TTE) revolve around academic excellence and specialization.[46] In contrast, biblical goals are more focused on forming charismatic practitioners capable of fulfilling Jesus's mission.[47] In describing the instructional methodology of TTE, Ruthven says:

> The format is characterized by the presentation of information rather than training; the information is depersonalized—as easily learned from a video as from a live teacher. The information deals with issues rarely if ever encountered in real ministry, but instead reflects tradition or the academic interests of the instructor. The knowledge tends to intimidate rather than edify; it can be intellectually exciting, but spiritually empty. And the knowledge is powerless when facing serious spiritual need; it evokes a vaguely guilty, uncomfortable feeling in the presence of God.[48]

Ruthven then contrasts the more impersonal, esoteric, abstract content and methodology of TTE with what Scripture presents as its method and content of training for ministry:

> The Biblical model of teaching modalities for Christian workers is characterized by: 1) a significant NT emphasis on the process, 2) implementing a highly-charismatic expression of ministry skills or giftings, 3) within settings of actual ministry, 4) primarily by means of mentoring relationships.[49]

Melvin Hodges stresses that "workers should be trained to the task, not away from it."[50] Removing students from a ministry setting for the purpose of ministry training (in effect creating a training bubble) increases the risk of divorcing training from the realities of ministry. Preparation for ministry should be on-the-job training.

---

45. Ruthven, *What's Wrong*, 243–68.
46. Ruthven, *What's Wrong*, 255–59.
47. Ruthven, *What's Wrong*, 254–55.
48. Ruthven, *What's Wrong*, 259.
49. Ruthven, *What's Wrong*, 259–60; Rowdon, "Theological Education," 86.
50. Hodges, *Indigenous Church*, 61.

The classroom has the potential to make a valuable contribution to this kind of learning process and experience. There, students can take advantage of the opportunity to learn and develop from hands on experiences as they debrief by interacting with fellow students and instructors.[51] An even greater level of useful knowledge about how to serve effectively can be gained through experiences, both negative and positive, if those experiences happen within a ministering community. Implicit in this entire view of training is a mentoring process designed to result in effective spiritual leaders.[52]

CONCLUSION

How can schools structure themselves, their training content, process, etc. to facilitate the formation of the qualities prescribed by Paul in their students? Here is a list of suggested questions for self-evaluation:

1. What qualities do we want to see in our graduates?

2. What is the basis for determining what qualities we want to see in our graduates?

3. To what extent do we design training processes and curriculum based on other than biblical perspectives and prescriptions?

4. To what extent do extrabiblical perspectives on our training processes and curriculum help or hinder us in forming the kinds of leaders we desire? To what extent are these perspectives neutral?

5. How often do we self-evaluate the effectiveness of our training? What are the criteria for our self-evaluation?

---

51. Conserman, "Assessment of Ministry Formation," 123. Gaining greater confidence to minister, in addition to sharpening ministry skills and gifts, is another benefit of training to the task.

52. Elliston, *Home Grown Leaders*, 132.

Unit 3: Training

Chapter 6

The Training Process in Scripture

INTRODUCTION

SCRIPTURE GIVES MANY EXAMPLES of leadership development. The patterns and underlying principles are relevant to training Spirit-filled leaders for the local church today. The importance of the preparation of spiritual leaders for the twenty-first century cannot be overstated. The foundational understanding of what leaders and leadership for the church are, along with the content and process of their training, must be informed by Scripture.[1]

From the OT, this chapter examines the preparation of prophets, priests, and kings who were to provide leadership for the Israelites. From the NT, it explores Jesus's training of the Twelve from the Gospel of Mark and Paul's mentoring of Timothy from Acts and Paul's Epistles. I will then summarize important characteristics that seem to be priorities of the process described in Scripture.[2]

OLD TESTAMENT LEADERSHIP DEVELOPMENT

Three general types of leaders in the OT filled the primary leadership roles: prophets, priests, and kings. This chapter briefly examines the preparation of these kinds of leaders and their transition into leadership. It also notes

---

1. Banks, *Reenvisioning Theological Education*, 71–126.
2. Banks, *Reenvisioning Theological Education*, 77–78.

how that information relates to the formation of Spirit-filled leaders for the local church today.

Prophets

Prophets understood themselves to be divinely called, and not just as people with a profession or skill.[3] A call narrative describing how individuals became prophets can be discerned by the following: an experience of God's dynamic working ("The word of the Lord came to . . ."), a divine designation as a prophet, the prophet's response to the call (often beginning as an objection), and divine reassurance to overcome the objection.[4]

Moses, based on Deut 18:15–19 and 34:10, was seen as a "standard of comparison" for OT prophets.[5] In contrast to a sovereign, divine call, one mark of false prophets was to personally initiate a prophetic ministry.[6]

While the OT focuses primarily on individual prophets, it also mentions schools of the prophets and groups of prophets.[7] Seeing the negative results of weak spiritual leadership, Samuel established schools of the prophets as he itinerated throughout Israel. These schools were located in Bethel, Gilgal, Ramah, Jericho, and other places.[8] There may be parallels between these and theological colleges of recent centuries.[9] In the schools of the prophets, students studied the law and its interpretation, along with "music and sacred poetry, both of which had been connected with prophecy from the time of Moses (Ex 15:20) and the judges (Jgs. 4:4; 5:1)."[10] Passages like 2 Kgs 9:1–3 indicate that students also carried out ministry assignments for the prophets who led them. As such, these locations were more than just training centers; they were ministry centers where members maintained a long-term association.[11]

---

3. Stevens, *Leadership Roles*, 33.

4. Stevens, *Leadership Roles,* 44–47.

5. Hoad, "Prophecy and Prophets."

6. Hoad, "Prophecy and Prophets."

7. 1 Sam 19:18–24; 2 Kgs 2:3, 5, 7, 15. Group of prophets, 1 Sam 10:5, 10; company of prophets, 1 Sam 19:20; large groups of prophets, 1 Kgs 18:4; sons of the prophets, 1 Kgs 20:35; 2 Kgs 4:1, 38; 5:22; 6:1; 9:1.

8. Elwell and Comfort, "Samuel," in *Tyndale Bible Dictionary.*

9. Unger, "Prophet," in *Unger's Bible Dictionary.*

10. Unger, "Prophet," in *Unger's Bible Dictionary.*

11. Unger, "Schools, Hebrew," in *Unger's Bible Dictionary*; Banks, *Reenvisioning*

Encounters with the Spirit were a part of the prophets' experience.[12] Saul met groups of prophets engaged in musical expression and prophecy (1 Sam 10:5, 10). Contagious prophecy, attributed to the Spirit, apparently passed from groups of prophets to Saul and his representatives (1 Sam 19:20–24).[13]

Priests

For those born into the tribe of Levi, priesthood was normally entered based on heredity, if the candidate was not disqualified by some physical defect or disfigurement.[14] There were also cases like Samuel, where boys not descended from the priestly tribe functioned as priests or Levites.[15]

Throughout the OT period, the priesthood served purposes in various areas of life,[16] so only general observations can be made about it. Those broad areas were sacrifice, purification, divination (prophecy or interpreting God's will), and teaching the law.[17] Training content would prepare them for these kinds of service. These responsibilities and references to training may give some understanding of what their training consisted of. Variations in these things were dependent on the period of history and situation of those in the priestly line.[18]

Samuel's early experiences give indications of priesthood training. For him, it began at the age of two or three years, as soon as he was weaned by his mother and brought to Eli.[19] His serving before Eli (1 Sam 2:11) could be understood as an apprenticeship, where he learned the information

---

Theological Education, 87–88.

12. Horton, *What the Bible Says*, 48–49. I view these experiences as legitimate encounters with the same Holy Spirit who is described as working throughout the OT and NT.

13. Jamieson et al., *Commentary Critical*, 1:188.

14. Unger, "Priesthood, Hebrew," in *Unger's Bible Dictionary*

15. Stevens, *Leadership Roles*, 65; Banks, *Reenvisioning Theological Education*, 86.

16. Distinctions and commonalities between the priesthood and Levites are beyond the scope of this study.

17. Stevens, *Leadership Roles*, 68–85.

18. For example, if there was no tabernacle or temple, or if they were part of the diaspora, priests might not learn about or carry out sacrificial responsibilities. Rudimentary medical practice might be connected with purification. Instruction in the law was dependent on having memorized the Torah or the availability of a written copy.

19. R. Smith, *Samuel*, 12–13.

and developed the skills needed to serve as a priest (1 Sam 2:11). There may have also been a group of dedicated women who helped to train and care for the young child.[20] Samuel's failure to recognize God's voice (1 Sam 3:1–14) indicates that the pneumatic aspects of priesthood were not a part of his training.[21]

Kings

To reign as king in Israel was to exercise God's authority on earth.[22] God chose their kings, but the people also participated in the selection process.[23]

The long season of preparation that David experienced before he began his reign over a united Israel[24] serves as an ideal for the preparation of monarchs. It is remarkable that David, as he confronted Goliath, seemed to recognize that earlier tests of his skills and courage were part of a process to prepare him for future challenges and opportunities (1 Sam 17:34–37). His informal preparation was holistic, including pneumatic experiences and character development, learning of political and military strategy, growth in relational and administrative skills, and so on.[25] It is notable that the description of David's extended time of preparation and qualification for leadership is in sharp contrast to very little attention given to the preparation of Saul.[26]

David's final instructions to Solomon imply that Solomon was taught the law (1 Kgs 2:1–4). His visions or dreams indicate familiarity with pneumatic experience (1 Kgs 3:1–15). His ability to judge difficult cases indicates the practical application of wisdom learned at a younger age (vv. 16–28).[27]

---

20. R. Smith, *Samuel*, 40–41.

21. R. Smith, *Samuel*, 65–66. Smith notes that the lack of instruction in this area likely motivated Samuel to establish schools of the prophets.

22. Stevens, *Leadership Roles*, 10.

23. Stevens, *Leadership Roles*, 10–14.

24. Unger, "David," in *Unger's Bible Dictionary*. King David's first seven and a half years were over a divided Israel.

25. This stage in David's life began in 1 Sam 16:12 and continued through 2 Sam 4.

26. Elliston, *Home Grown Leaders*, 45.

27. The contrast between the eventual heir of the throne, Solomon, and the attempted usurper of the throne, Absalom, is striking. Although the contrast is beyond the scope of this study, it would be worthwhile to examine how each was treated and instructed as a child and youth.

One apparent purpose for the book of Proverbs is to give guidance to those who exercise political or civil authority.[28] While there were successes and failures in the Davidic line, the ideal was that emerging political leaders be taught the Torah and apply it in personal life and rule. One notable example of this was the high priest Jehoiada and the six-year preparation of young Jehoash (2 Kgs 11:3; 2 Chron 22:11–12).

Pneumatic Experience and Human Development

Pentecostals and charismatics sometimes see spiritual leaders as larger than life because of their public persona or the distinctiveness of their ministry.[29] This view has led to personal and ministerial failure in well-known and highly regarded ministers.[30]

Based on his examination of the experiences of Samson, Saul, and David, Wonsuk Ma argues that each of these OT leaders passed through a stage of personal development and transformation. This stage contained both dynamic and mundane aspects. It occurred between the initial call to leadership and the leader's emergence into the position and the public recognition of his leadership.[31] This temporal gap was necessary to form the emerging leader's character and to develop the skills he would need.[32] There is an important implication here that bears on ministerial training:

> Education and training, although quite "human" in process, are nonetheless intended by God to be an essential preparation for God's workers. In fact, this "natural" process is an equal counterpart of the "supernatural" experience of the leaders with the Spirit. What was expected during the temporal gap between the initial coming of the Spirit for inner impact and the "empowerment" of the Spirit for a task? This must be the "natural" process in mundane and routine surroundings. Here we find the validity of training and education in God's economy. Therefore, the educational or developmental process should encompass the whole spectrum of

28. Deane and Taylor-Taswell, *Proverbs*, 1; Arnold and Beyer, *Encountering the Old Testament*, 317–18.

29. See Ma, "Charismatic Leadership," 285; Ma, "Tragedy of Spirit-Empowered Heroes," 115–31.

30. See Ma, "Charismatic Leadership," 285–86.

31. Ma, "Charismatic Leadership," 288–97.

32. Ma, "Charismatic Leadership," 298.

human development, including spiritual, mental, emotional, intellectual, relational, and physical.[33]

Training institutions provide a setting where much of the formative and developmental purpose of this temporal gap can be fulfilled. Students' training experience should encompass both the dynamic experiences and the mundane routines and disciplines necessary to prepare them to step into the areas of ministry that God has called them to fill.

Leadership Transition

Five elements were vital to the success of OT leadership transition: "source of authority, Divine approval or disapproval, transfer of power, popular recognition or rejection, and the relationship between the older and the younger leader."[34] After examining the successful transitions from Moses to Joshua, Elijah to Elisha, Eli to Samuel, and the abortive transition from Eli to his sons, Kay Fountain summarizes four principles for leadership transition. First, God makes clear who is his choice and who carries divine authority. Second, there is an unambiguous, public declaration of the choice of the new leader and delegation of authority. Third, over an extended period, the emerging leader learns by experience how to lead by serving.[35] Fourth, at a specific point in time, power is publicly transferred to the new leader.[36] Although Fountain focuses on the transition from missionary to national leadership at the denominational level, these principles apply to preparing the emerging generation of leaders. Ministerial education is a vital part of leadership transition in any renewal movement. The process and content of training are especially relevant to Fountain's first three principles: to confirm God's call on individuals, to include public recognition, and to form students into servant leaders.

---

33. Ma, "Charismatic Leadership," 301.

34. See Fountain, "Investigation," 252.

35. See Fountain, "Investigation," 276. Fountain observes, "It is clear, however, that these three men succeeded their masters not only because of the things they learned in observing their masters, but also because of the servant attitude which developed in each of them. They were not servants for a few days, weeks, or months. They were all servants for a considerable portion of their youth, and perhaps even adult life."

36. See Fountain, "Investigation," 274–77.

Summary of Summary of Old Testament Leadership Development

Four principles appear to be common to the development of OT leaders and the preparation of Spirit-filled local church leaders. First, there is a divine call that people recognize and acknowledge. Those who seek training should have some awareness of a divine call. Throughout the training process, recognized and ratified by others, students should expect to receive a clearer understanding of the particulars of their call.[37] Second, students and educators should expect the Holy Spirit to work through the training process and content, in what is intentionally built into it and in spontaneous ways.[38] Third, both the process of training and its content are needed. Those involved in training must do everything possible to ensure that both parts contribute to the ultimate goal of forming Spirit-filled leaders. Fourth, training must be holistic in nature, preparing the whole person for spiritual leadership.

NEW TESTAMENT LEADERSHIP DEVELOPMENT

Jesus's Training of the Twelve

Many aspects of the Twelve's experiences with Jesus can help us to reflect on leadership training.[39] Information from the Gospels does not fit neatly into categories of twenty-first-century thinking, but it gives sufficient insight to inform educators. I will briefly overview pertinent concepts.

Longenecker, basing his work on the research of Robert Meye in the Gospel of Mark,[40] breaks down Jesus's discipleship and training process

---

37. In some cases, students considering training or already involved in it may not feel absolutely certain of a call to ministry or of the specifics of their call. Because of the great variety of ways in which people experience an awareness of a call to ministry, much flexibility should be exercised in discerning how God is working in this area of students' lives.

38. Process involves the experiences of the student. Content involves what educators expect the student to learn, understand, and apply. Throughout the process, this should become clearer to students and educators.

39. In examining possible correlations, educators must keep an important qualification in mind. In the Gospels, the training of the Twelve took place in the context of the unfolding of Jesus's redemptive work. Now, training takes place with the NT church being a reality and in the context of the ongoing participation of the church in the Great Commission.

40. Meye, *Jesus and the Twelve*.

into four phases. In each one, Jesus reproduces in the Twelve a quality that would enable them to lead the infant church: a living faith (Mark 1:1–3:19); dynamic personal growth (3:20–9:29); relational competence (9:30–10:52); and vision (11:1–16:20).[41] Longenecker describes the specific elements of this process: a servant leader who models the envisioned result; genuine, transparent relationships between the leader and each follower; a bonded group whose members can relate to facilitate wholeness and maturity; and discipling.[42] He contrasts this mentoring and discipling with professional instruction and describes it as taking place "under the influence of long association with a few significant and admired persons."[43]

After describing the interaction of these elements in the various phases, Longenecker explains that this was not a process that could be neatly compartmentalized during Jesus's ministry or brought to completion at the end of Mark. There would be continued seasons of refining leaders' lives and guiding them through a myriad of difficult situations and processes.[44]

A. B. Bruce[45] goes into greater detail than Longenecker and offers helpful insights that supplement our understanding of Longenecker's four phases. I will limit this study to Bruce's observations about the Gospel of Mark and will use those observations to formulate relevant views.

The Four Phases

Believing (Mark 1:1—3:19)

A quick reading of the text where Peter, Andrew, James, and John were called to follow Jesus (Mark 1:16–20) might give the impression that they were not previously aware of Jesus and that this call came abruptly. However, these men probably had some knowledge of and acquaintance with Jesus already.[46] The healing of Peter's mother-in-law was a compelling

---

41. Longenecker, *Growing Leaders by Design*, 42. See also Banks, *Reenvisioning Theological Education*, 104–6, where he gives a snapshot of Jesus's training process from the events recorded in Mark 8–10.

42. Longenecker, *Growing Leaders by Design*, 30–34.

43. Longenecker, *Growing Leaders by Design*, 34.

44. Longenecker, *Growing Leaders by Design*, 68–69.

45. A. Bruce, *Training of the Twelve*.

46. A. Bruce, *Training of the Twelve*, 13–14.

experience that personally affected him (vv. 29–31) and was another part of the process.

Peter and Andrew may not have been as economically well-off as James and John, who had hired servants assisting them (Mark 1:20).[47] As a tax collector, Matthew was wealthy (2:14–15).[48] It appears that the Twelve represented a relatively broad demographic spectrum, in terms of the contemporary society,[49] and that Jesus's choice of Matthew illustrates that he did not make a person's past or others' view of that person the basis of choosing him for leadership.[50]

After apparently spending the night in prayer, Jesus called the Twelve from among the larger group of his disciples (Mark 3:13–19). In all of Scripture, selection of spiritual leaders is based firmly on a sovereign divine call. Volunteerism and other positive characteristics in volunteers for leadership are not undesirable, but are insufficient: "While integrity is always important, and the qualifications, commitment, situation, status and other traits are often brought into focus, another consistent, essential component in the selection process is 'God's calling.'"[51]

Growing (Mark 3:20—9:29)

This phase was the most active season of Jesus's ministry, with much travel and ministry activity.[52] Jesus warmly affirmed the commitment of the Twelve to him (Mark 3:31–35). They grew in their understanding of Jesus's teaching through hearing both the parables and their interpretation (4:1–34). After observing Jesus's ministry of healing and deliverance (5:1–43), they were sent out to preach, heal, and deliver, thus developing their practical ministry skills (6:7–32).

There were also negative experiences. They observed and felt the pain of Jesus's rejection at Nazareth (Mark 6:1–6). Jesus rebuked them for not recognizing the depth of evil that was arrayed against him and his mission

47. A. Bruce, *Training of the Twelve*, 16.

48. A. Bruce, *Training of the Twelve*, 17–22.

49. Banks, *Reenvisioning Theological Education*, 113–14. Paul appears to have worked with an even broader demographic of ministry associates.

50. A. Bruce, *Training of the Twelve*, 17. This variety was not limited to economic status. There was also a broad political and social variety represented among the Twelve.

51. Elliston, *Home Grown Leaders*, 46.

52. A. Bruce, *Training of the Twelve*, 28–92.

(8:14–21).[53] After affirming Peter's confession of him as the Christ, Jesus strongly rebuked Peter for prioritizing self-preservation over submission to God's will, after Jesus announced his coming sufferings and death (8:31–33).[54] The exhilaration of the transfiguration with Peter, James, and John was followed by two failures. The first involved the inability of the disciples to cast out a demon (9:14–29). The second, described below, led into the next phase of their training.

Relating (Mark 9:30—10:52)

Introducing this section, Bruce observes:

> Men may have made great progress in the art of prayer, in religious liberty, in Christian activity, may have shown themselves faithful in times of temptation, and apt scholars in Christian doctrine, and yet prove signally defective in temper: self-willed, self-seeking, having an eye to their own glory, even when seeking to glorify God. Most needful, for what good could these disciples do as ministers of the kingdom so long as their main concern was about their own place therein?[55]

A vital part of the training process was balancing understanding of Jesus's teaching and practical skills with the right regard for people. This was the priority of the relating phase of training.

Twice during the final journey to Jerusalem, Jesus spoke to the disciples about his upcoming suffering and death (Mark 9:30–37; 10:35–45).[56] After each warning, Mark reports a discussion about position in the coming kingdom. The first was speculation among the disciples about greatness. The second was a request from the mother of James and John that her sons be given a special place. Besides the inappropriateness of her request and the disciples' conversation, they all seemed unaware of what the inevitable result would be: dissention and competition. Bruce draws a contrast between what is required to rule or lead. In human institutions, "they rule whose privilege it is to be ministered unto; in the divine commonwealth, they rule who account it a privilege to minister."[57]

53. A. Bruce, *Training of the Twelve*, 89–92.
54. A. Bruce, *Training of the Twelve*, 101.
55. A. Bruce, *Training of the Twelve*, 112.
56. A. Bruce, *Training of the Twelve*, 111–16, 156–58.
57. A. Bruce, *Training of the Twelve*, 162.

This section contains lessons about how to relate to one another and to others. Others include those also doing God's work but not associated with them (Mark 9:38–41);[58] those not highly valued, such as children (10:13–16); and persons with disabilities (vv. 46–52).

Aspiring (Mark 11:1—16:20)

The disciples witnessed confrontations between Jesus and the Jewish leaders who opposed him (Mark 11:27–33; 12:13–27, 35–40). Instead of being intimidated, Jesus maintained the initiative in debates with those seeking to destroy his credibility. The same coalitions would oppose the disciples in the future as they led the infant church.

Jesus's disciples also observed how Jesus responded to others who had various levels of sincerity (Mark 10:17–22; 12:28–34). He led such individuals to a moment of clarity about themselves and their response to him.

The disciples learned an unforgettable lesson about self-abandonment for God's purpose (Mark 14:3–9).[59] What appeared to be an irresponsible act—anointing Jesus with perfume worth a small fortune—reflected Jesus's sacrifice on the cross and expressed sincere worship that would be immortalized in the Gospels.[60]

Jesus's eschatological discourse in Mark 13 emphasized the need to remain constantly alert and ready. Through this, the disciples learned to stay watchful and aware of the ultimacy and seriousness of their call.[61]

Although the disciples were now in the final phase of their training with Jesus, their reactions to the unfolding events in Gethsemane (Mark 14:32–50) betray areas of profound deficiency. They lacked inward strength and courage, forethought and clear perception of the truth, knowledge of themselves, and the discipline that comes only from experience.[62] Peter's lack of experiential wisdom was especially demonstrated in the courtyard of the high priest (vv. 66–72).[63]

---

58. The strong warning in Mark 9:42–49 against prejudiced attitudes like this is notable.

59. A. Bruce, *Training of the Twelve*, 169–70, 175–76.

60. A. Bruce, *Training of the Twelve*, 169–70, 175–76.

61. A. Bruce, *Training of the Twelve*, 187–88.

62. A. Bruce, *Training of the Twelve*, 257–59.

63. A. Bruce, *Training of the Twelve*, 267–68

The angel's directive to the women at Jesus's tomb informing the disciples "and Peter" to meet Jesus in Galilee is remarkable (Mark 16:7). Only Mark's Gospel mentions this singling out of Peter, yet Mark gives no description of any private meeting between Jesus and Peter.[64]

Jesus's instruction at the institution of the Lord's Supper (Mark 14:22–26) was the clearest explanation he gave to the disciples about his saving work.[65] It was only after the resurrection that the disciples could grow in their understanding of the gospel and in their ability to proclaim it.[66] This valley experience was a necessary part of the preparation for the work that Jesus would commission them to do.[67] The commission (Mark 16:14–18)[68] was given only at the appropriate time—after the needed training process and Jesus's redemptive work were completed.[69]

Summary of Jesus and the Twelve

The believing phase mentioned above seems to mirror the pre-training or preparatory season for those who desire ministry training. It corresponds to a student's experiences and preparation through the local church—both the mundane processes and dynamic experiences that are a part of preparing those called to ministry. It also reflects a relatively broad demographic who are called to leadership.

The growing phase highlights two well-known parts of training: acquisition of knowledge and experience and development of ministry skills. It also includes character formation through various challenging situations and transformation through more dynamic experiences.

In the relating phase, those preparing for ministry continue to increase their knowledge and skills and to recognize the uniqueness and value of their spiritual gifts. At the same time, there is the risk of developing an

---

64. A. Bruce, *Training of the Twelve*, 274. "We can have no doubt at all as to its object. The Risen Master remembered Peter's sin; He knew how troubled he was in mind on account of it; He desired without delay to let him know he was forgiven; and out of delicate consideration for the offender's feelings He contrived to meet him for the first time after his fall, alone."

65. A. Bruce, *Training of the Twelve*, 197.

66. A. Bruce, *Training of the Twelve*, 276–77.

67. A. Bruce, *Training of the Twelve*, 278.

68. See Fountain, "Investigation," 277. This commissioning of the Eleven can be considered a parallel to the OT public commissioning of leaders.

69. A. Bruce, *Training of the Twelve*, 295.

arrogant or self-promoting attitude. Jesus primarily addressed this negative tendency at this stage of training.

The aspiring phase was the final step in Jesus's earthly ministry to prepare the Twelve to behave in a trustworthy and faithful manner. It could succeed only with a deeper level of transformation than the one that had occurred in earlier phases. The Twelve needed a more profound and honest confrontation with themselves, a more complete understanding of the message, and a more comprehensive encounter with Jesus than ever before.

THE FIRST-CENTURY APOSTOLIC CHURCH

Paul's Training and Mentoring of Timothy

The Challenge

While Paul's mentorship of Timothy provides principles for Spirit-filled ministerial training, this section presents a challenge similar to leadership training in the OT. In contrast to Mark, who makes the training process more visible, the purposes of the writers of Acts and of the Pauline church and pastoral epistles[70] are not directly related to ministerial training. In examining where Timothy is mentioned in Acts and other pertinent passages, I will highlight information that may indicate or reflect his experiences as a protégé of Paul.[71]

Acts

CONVERSION

Differing views exist about Timothy's conversion. Some scholars believe that his conversion took place through Paul's ministry during his first visit to Lystra and Derbe (Acts 14:6–23).[72] Others believe it was through the influence of his mother Eunice and grandmother Lois (2 Tim 1:5; 3:14–15).[73]

---

70. I assume Pauline authorship of all NT writings traditionally attributed to him.

71. Lawless, "Paul and Leadership Development," 216–34.

72. Unger, "Timothy," in *Unger's Bible Dictionary*.

73. Wiersbe, *Bible Exposition Commentary*, 2:241.

It is unclear whether Timothy and Paul were acquainted before Paul's return to Lystra (Acts 16:1–3), when he invited Timothy to join the team.[74]

JOINING PAUL

When Paul returned to Lystra two or three years after his first visit,[75] he desired and requested[76] to bring Timothy along (Acts 16:1–3). Luke mentions that the believers thought highly of Timothy and spoke well of him. In Paul's absence, Timothy had grown as a disciple and had demonstrated the kind of character that the believers in Lystra and Iconium could endorse.[77]

Although the time of Timothy's ordination for ministry remains unclear, it was likely when Paul requested him to accompany him.[78] His ordination was a significant experience to which Paul repeatedly referred (1 Tim 1:18–19; 4:14; 6:12;[79] 2 Tim 1:6, 14).

If Timothy was selected to replace Mark (Acts 12:25; 13:5, 13), then he would have assisted Paul and Silas in practical ways, as Joshua had done for Moses and Elisha for Elijah.[80] However, Bruce suggests that at least part of Mark's service to them was to provide firsthand information about Jesus.[81] While practical assistance could have been part of Paul's motivation for adding Timothy to the team, it proved to be a strategic selection:

> Perhaps the best thing that happened at Lystra was the enlistment of Timothy to replace John Mark as Paul's special assistant. . . . In the years that followed, Timothy played an important part in the expansion and strengthening of the churches. He traveled with

---

74. Pollock, *Apostle*, 89–90. Pollock believes Timothy accompanied and ministered to Paul and Barnabas when they left the area and traveled to Pamphylia (Acts 14:23–25).

75. F. Bruce, *Book of Acts*, 321.

76. "Thelo."

77. Conserman, "Assessment of Ministry Formation," 88–90. Conserman brings up the challenge that traditional Bible schools sometimes face with young students' emotional and social immaturity. Timothy's experience demonstrates how a student's home church can help a potential student work to advance in these vital areas and can vouch for the student's preparedness for the next part of the training process.

78. F. Bruce, *Book of Acts*, 323.

79. 1 Timothy 6:12 could be a reference to Timothy's conversion rather than his ordination.

80. Hervey, *Acts*, 402.

81. F. Bruce, *Book of Acts*, 263.

Paul and was often his special ambassador to the "trouble spots" in the work, such as Corinth.[82]

In Macedonia

Luke does not mention Timothy during the first season of travel and ministry with Paul and Silas (Acts 16:4–17:13). No doubt the two conversed, and Timothy observed. During this time, Paul's missionary team distributed the Jerusalem leaders' letter to the churches (Acts 15:23–29; 16:4–5) and sought direction for where to go (with prohibitions from the Spirit about going to some places). This was a valuable time for Timothy to establish relationships and learn more about charismatic ministry.

Luke does not mention Timothy's part in the remarkable founding of the church in Philippi. When Paul and Silas left Philippi, the text seems to favor the view that Timothy stayed there and later met Paul in Berea.[83] Timothy and Luke[84] apparently stayed there for a short time to follow up before proceeding to meet Paul in Berea.[85]

When Paul was forced to leave Berea (Acts 17:14), he left Silas and Timothy there, probably to follow up as they had done in Philippi. He instructed them to join him as soon as possible in Athens. They apparently met in Corinth instead of Athens, although Timothy may have come to Athens and been sent to Thessalonica by Paul (1 Thess 3:1–2).[86]

In Greece

After rejoining Paul in Corinth (Acts 18:5) to assist with the work there, Timothy is not mentioned again until about five years later,[87] when Paul is ready to leave Ephesus (Acts 19:22). Paul sends him with Erastus to Macedonia to prepare the churches for Paul's upcoming visit (1 Cor 4:17; 16:10).

82. Wiersbe, *Bible Exposition Commentary,* 1: 467.

83. Luke's focus is on Paul and Silas throughout the entire account of the founding of the Philippian church. It seems logical that when they departed (*exelthontes*) and left the brethren at Lydia's home that Luke was still referring only to Paul and Silas.

84. Luke had apparently joined them in Troas (note the transition from *they* to *we* in Acts 16:6–10).

85. Wiersbe, *Bible Exposition Commentary,* 1:471.

86. Toussaint, *Bible Knowledge Commentary,* 2:402.

87. Unger, "Timothy," in *Unger's Bible Dictionary*

Paul plans to encourage the congregations and to receive the funds they had promised for the relief of the needy believers in Jerusalem.[88] He spends three months in Greece, and possibly a year in Macedonia.[89] Interestingly, in Acts 19:22, Timothy and Erastus are described as those who minister to (*diakonountōn*) Paul. Luke's use of this term seems to indicate serving in practical ways.[90]

The final mention of Timothy in Acts is in 20:1–6. He, along with representatives from the various churches in Macedonia, Pamphylia, and Asia Minor, join Paul in Troas to carry the offerings from their churches to the impoverished believers living in Judea.

Paul's Church Epistles

Paul mentions Timothy being with him or representing him in many of his letters to churches. They are together in Corinth when Paul writes Romans (Rom 16:21);[91] in Ephesus and Macedonia, when Paul is writing 1 and 2 Corinthians (1 Cor 4:17; 16:10; 2 Cor 1:1, 19);[92] in Rome, while Paul is writing Philippians (Phil 1:1; 2:19)[93] and Colossians (Col 1:1);[94] and in Corinth, when Paul is writing 1 Thessalonians (1 Thess 1:1; 3:1–2, 6)[95] and 2 Thessalonians (2 Thess 1:1).[96]

The most affectionate and lengthy description Paul gives of Timothy is in Phil 2:19–22. His words reflect the fruit of an intentional investment in the life of an emerging spiritual leader:

> But I hope in the Lord Jesus to send Timothy to you shortly, so that I also may be encouraged when I learn of your condition. For I have no one else of kindred spirit who will genuinely be concerned

88. F. Bruce, *Book of Acts*, 394.

89. F. Bruce, *Book of Acts*, 404–5.

90. "Diakoneo."

91. Unger, "Romans, Epistle to," in *Unger's Bible Dictionary*.

92. Unger, "Corinthians, First Epistle," and "Corinthians, Second Epistle," in *Unger's Bible Dictionary*.

93. Unger, "Philippians, Epistle to," in *Unger's Bible Dictionary*.

94. Unger, "Colossians, Book of," in *Unger's Bible Dictionary*.

95. Unger, "Thessalonians, First Epistle to," in *Unger's Bible Dictionary*.

96. Jamieson et al., *Commentary Critical*, 2:393. Although there is disagreement about time and place of writing, it seems most natural that 2 Thessalonians was written from Corinth around six months after 1 Thessalonians.

for your welfare. For they all seek after their own interests, not those of Christ Jesus. But you know of his proven worth, that he served with me in the furtherance of the gospel like a child serving his father.

1 and 2 Timothy

Collegial Relationship

The Pastoral Epistles were not written to students preparing for ministry, but to younger ministry colleagues.[97] Thus they have a collegial tone that reflects how Paul and Timothy's relationship had progressed over the years. Timothy is now a colleague of Paul and not in a subordinate or teacher-student relationship with him.[98] One example of this is at the beginning of 1 Timothy, which begins with an exhortation (1 Tim 1:3) that is more of an appeal than a command.[99]

Requirements for Spiritual Leadership

Something notable about the requirements for an overseer, elder, or bishop (*episkopes*) in 1 Tim 3:1–7 is that they prioritize observable character traits.[100] One might ask whether these character traits should be expected to develop apart from a process, or whether the training process should serve as a means through which these traits are formed and reinforced. If forming or reinforcing these qualities was part of Paul's aim in mentoring Timothy, this factor should inform the processes, content, and objective of ministerial training.

---

97. Jamieson et al., *Commentary Critical,* 2:401.

98. Banks, *Reenvisioning Theological Education,* 114–17.

99. Jamieson et al., *Commentary Critical,* 2:404. Paul urged (*parekalesa*) him to remain at Ephesus.

100. Gibbs, "Training Pyramid," 128. Such traits are prioritized somewhat over knowledge or skills but not to their exclusion. For example, teaching or managing a household are skills, while being temperate, prudent, and respectable are character traits. See also the charts in ch. 5 of this book, "The Development of Spiritual Leaders."

CONTINUAL GROWTH

First Timothy 4 encourages continued growth. In verse 6, Timothy is to be constantly nourished (*entrephomenos*) in the objective truth of the faith and the doctrine he has followed. In 4:14–16, he must not neglect his spiritual gift,[101] but be absorbed and make observable progress in it. As he perseveres in these things, there is great potential for advancing God's saving purpose. Wiersbe notes:

> "Meditate" carried the idea of "be in them, give yourself totally to them." Timothy's spiritual life and ministry were to be the absorbing, controlling things in his life, not merely sidelines that he occasionally practiced. There can be no real pioneer advance in one's ministry without total dedication to the task.[102]

TEACHING

Although the character and lifestyle described in 1 Tim 3:1–7 are required of overseers, 2 Tim 1:13 and Titus 2:2 indicate that teaching and instruction are equally indispensable. Paul had given this wholesome teaching[103] to Timothy and expected him to pass it on to others who would then continue to teach others.[104]

OBSERVATION

Paul's training of Timothy also contained elements of observation. In 2 Tim 2:24–26, Paul instructs Timothy about dealing with those who need correction. The qualities listed there (kindness, ability to teach, patience and gentleness, and not being contentious), were ones Timothy witnessed as he served with Paul. At the same time, Timothy could observe firsthand as his mentor Paul grew in these areas. In 2 Tim 3:10–11, Paul specifically

---

101. While it is uncertain exactly what this gift was, it is sufficient to the purpose of this study to know that it was related to overseeing the congregation.

102. Wiersbe, *Bible Exposition Commentary,* 2:228.

103. "Giano." Wholesome (*ygiainonton*) teaching is Paul's prescription to overcome false teaching.

104. It should be noted that this teaching is much more than imparting information or skills. It is formational and transformational.

reminds Timothy about what he had observed of his "teaching, conduct, purpose, faith, patience, love, perseverance, persecutions, and sufferings."

ORDINATION

Paul refers repeatedly to Timothy's ordination (1 Tim 1:18–19; 4:14; 6:12; 2 Tim 1:6, 14), a significant event in his life because of the aspects Paul mentions. It was pneumatic, with prophetic utterances given and a bestowal of *charismatos* through the laying on of hands.[105] It was a public commissioning. It recognized ministry as a sacred trust (*paratheken*), a God-given deposit that the minister must guard through the work of the Spirit.

PRE-TRAINING PREPARATION

A final ingredient in Timothy's experience is mentioned in 2 Tim 3:14–17. Paul recognizes that from infancy (*brephous*), Timothy had been taught the Scriptures (presumably by his mother and grandmother).[106] Regardless of the time and person(s) used by God in his conversion (Paul or Lois and Eunice), the elders' recommendation of Timothy (Acts 16:1–3) validated the importance of this stage of his development.

Summary of Paul and Timothy

Pre-training experiences and processes in Timothy's life were important to prepare him for and to confirm his readiness to be mentored by Paul. His family, church, and congregational leadership each played a part in this.

Paul saw training and even more so mentoring as a long-term process, including many parts. Some of those parts are observation; assignment of tasks and responsibilities; assisting in practical ways; increasing levels of responsibility; and being with and building relationships with mentors. Tim Tucker catches the concept of Paul's long-term commitment to mentor Timothy, observing that he "was intentional about developing relationships with younger leaders and supported them over many years,

---

105. The nature of this impartation through the laying on of hands is beyond the scope of this study.

106. Jamieson et al., *Commentary Critical*, 2:427.

providing both an example for them to follow, as well as ongoing support and encouragement."[107]

While the training process advances the knowledge and skills of the protégé, it seems to prioritize the formation of individuals who demonstrate specific, observable character traits and are committed to growth in those traits throughout their lifetime.[108] A public, charismatic commissioning or ordination event signifies the sacredness of the call to service and acknowledges the minister's obligation to persevere and guard his or her call.

CONCLUSION

A number of observations can be made from synthesizing the results of this survey of leadership development in Scripture. The following characteristics provide biblical priorities that should be in place for training Spirit-filled local church leaders for the twenty-first century.[109]

First, individuals' backgrounds and experiences are a vital part of their preparation for leadership training and entering into leadership.[110] OT leaders were to be nurtured in the home setting before entering into formal training. Timothy's home and church background provided a foundation for his entrance into ministry alongside Paul. The Twelve's knowledge of Jesus before he called them to follow him initially as disciples, along with various dynamic experiences or observations of his ministry, prepared them for the moment when he called them to follow him and ultimately to serve as leaders of the apostolic church.

Second, the work of the Spirit is characteristic throughout the entire process of the emerging leader's background, growing awareness of calling, and formation. This work of the Spirit is woven into the entire spectrum of experiences, from the most mundane and routine processes to the most dynamic and memorable moments. Although it is less visible in Mark's account of the training of Jesus's disciples, it is clear to see that the disciples were being transformed through all those parts of the process in which Jesus led them.[111]

---

107. Tucker, *Pacesetter*, 21.

108. Schreiner, *Paul*, 244.

109. Banks, *Reenvisioning Theological Education*, 126.

110. F. Clinton, *Making of a Leader*, 44.

111. Banks, *Reenvisioning Theological Education*, 104–6.

Third, the experiences of all reflect a holistic balance. On the one hand, leaders could develop the knowledge and skills necessary to perform leadership tasks. Additionally, they underwent a process of spiritual and character formation necessary for credibility and for becoming long-term servants and leaders. This process working in them provided a tangible, visible example for all to see of God's transformative process at work.

Fourth, all were in one form or another set apart and publicly recognized as God-called leaders. The public recognition and official placement into leadership took various forms. For OT leaders, there was often a civic or tribal/national gathering or convocation.[112] For Timothy, there was an ordination service, probably with the congregation and leadership of his church in Derbe or Lystra. For the Eleven, there was the series of events related to Jesus's resurrection and ascension, and then the day of Pentecost.

112. Because of the nature of their ministries, many of the OT prophets were not recognized by their contemporaries as legitimate prophets. However, their ministries and oral or written proclamation were ultimately vindicated.

Chapter 7

The Spirit in the Training Process

INTRODUCTION

THE HOLY SPIRIT TEACHES and reveals truth. He is actively involved in transforming the lives of believers into the image of Christ. Because of this, those who train local church leaders should expect him to work throughout the entirety of the teaching and learning process of their programs.

The Holy Spirit is central to the work of Christian teaching and is intimately involved in the process. This chapter surveys specific areas relative to his involvement. Two main areas of emphasis in this chapter relate to the Holy Spirit in the ministry training process.

First, I examine facets of the teaching gift and its relationship to ministry training. The NT describes Jesus as a charismatic teacher. Based on the characteristics and pattern of his teaching ministry, Jesus commissioned the apostolic church and following generations to continue the same kind of transformative teaching as they carried the gospel throughout the world (Acts 1:1–8).[1]

Second, I discuss Pentecostal/charismatic distinctives in the training process. The characteristics of these beliefs, values, and experiences and a contemporary continuation of this pneumatic ministry are to exemplify

---

1. Luke does not seem to distinguish the categories of doing, teaching, and witness. Is it possible that these aspects of ministry, especially when viewed as expressions of charismatic ministry, should be less rigorously separated or compartmentalized? See Ruthven, *What's Wrong*, 25, 152.

Christian teaching in general. These distinctives should then characterize the training of those called to lead the local church. A blend of spiritual experience, along with a holistic education that informs the mind and that forms both the character and skills for ministry, must rely on the hidden curriculum of the Spirit throughout the entire training process. These values work to ensure the long-term stability and growth of a renewal movement.

THE TEACHING GIFT

Jesus's Teaching Ministry

To introduce this aspect of ministerial training, it is important to briefly mention Jesus's teaching ministry, with observations here from Matthew's Gospel. The rationale for using Matthew is that his is the only Gospel that refers specifically to the church (*ekklesia*, Matt 16:18; 18:17), and he specifically emphasizes teaching as part of the Great Commission.[2]

Teaching with Authority

Matthew describes Jesus as teaching with authority (Matt 7:28–29), in contrast to the scribes, who derived authority from past teachers.[3] Jesus's authority was observable in both what he taught and how he taught.[4] This ultimately led to inquiries about the source of his authority (21:23). Additionally, Matthew ties teaching and healing together (4:23; 9:35). To add additional weight to the authoritative character of the teaching,[5] authority is linked with healing as an authentication of Jesus's identity as the prophet of Deut 18:15–19.[6]

---

2. Guthrie, *New Testament Introduction*, 30–31.

3. A. Williams, *Matthew*, 287.

4. Jamieson et al., *Commentary Critical*, 2:31.

5. Matthew adds preaching in 9:35.

6. Barbieri et al., *Bible Knowledge Commentary*, 2:28.

The Great Commission and Teaching

Matthew's Great Commission (Matt 28:18–20) is an expression of Jesus's universal authority (v. 18; *exousia*, as in 7:29). This universal authority is the basis of the Commission.[7] The use of "make disciples" (v. 19) and "teaching" (v. 20) emphasizes transformative instruction.[8] Craig Keener sees the fulfillment of the Great Commission happening through "multiplying the work by trusting the Holy Spirit and Christ's teaching to multiply equally committed laborers for the harvest."[9] The fulfillment of the Great Commission is thus inseparably linked to and dependent on the transformative teaching of grassroots disciples and the formation of those who will become the leaders of the local church.

The Pneumatic Aspect

Matthew uses the term Christ often in reference to Jesus, most notably in Matt 16:13–20.[10] If Christ is a charismatic designation, then Matthew seems to understand Jesus's teaching ministry to be pneumatic.[11] Although much debate has occurred about exactly how to understand Jesus's relationship with the Spirit, it seems clear enough that Jesus was anointed by the Spirit for his ministry, including teaching.[12]

Pneumatic Teaching in the Apostolic Church

The Spirit's role in Jesus's teaching points to his continuing activity through the transformative teaching gift in the apostolic church.[13] Paul's ministry reflected the high priority given to charismatic, transformative teaching.[14]

---

7. Barbieri et al., *Bible Knowledge Commentary*, 2:93.

8. Keener, "Matthew's Missiology," 3. Keener sees the Great Commission as a single mandate fulfilled in three ways: "The one command is to make disciples of the nations and this command is implemented by going, baptizing, and teaching."

9. Keener, "Matthew's Missiology," 15.

10. Matthew also uses the term Christ in direct or indirect reference to Jesus in 1:1, 16–18; 11:2; 16:16, 20; 22:42; 23:10; 26:63, 68; and 27:17, 22.

11. Horton, *What the Bible Says*, 95; Paffenroth, "Jesus as Anointed."

12. Stronstad, *Charismatic Theology*, 45–46, 58, 68, 81.

13. Rowdon, "Theological Education," 75.

14. Banks, *Reenvisioning Theological Education*, 117–21.

The NT passages relevant to teaching and spiritual gifts are Rom 12:6–8; 1 Cor 12:8–10, 27–30; 14:6, 26; Eph 4:7–11; and 1 Pet 4:10–11.[15] My purpose is not to examine spiritual gifts thoroughly[16] but to briefly examine teaching as it relates to spiritual gifts and to show its relevance to ministerial training.

Gifts Are Incarnational

It is an error to make too big a distinction between extraordinary, supernatural gifts and those that seem ordinary. The more charismatic gifts like prophecy and a word of wisdom or knowledge can be manifested in preaching and teaching.[17]

Spiritual gifts should be viewed as incarnational. They are not just well-developed natural human abilities or skills. They are also not totally supernatural, independent of any human factor in their manifestation. This means that when a believer willingly submits to the Holy Spirit, how the Spirit manifests himself reflects that person's specific characteristics.[18]

Ministry Gifts and Enabling Gifts

David Lim sees three categories of spiritual gifts listed in 1 Cor 12:8–10, based on the use and placement of *hallos* and *heteros*.[19] Teaching and preaching gifts that express the message of wisdom or of knowledge may be manifested in worship, but they should also be expected in settings where leaders are encouraging the people or leading them to grow spiritually.[20]

15. However, it may be that pneumatic, transformative teaching was understood by the apostolic church to have a much more significant place that is foundational to the work of the Spirit in the lives of believers and congregations than today's church realizes. See Ruthven, *What's Wrong*, 163–75.

16. For a thorough treatment, see for example Lim, "Spiritual Gifts"; Stronstad, *Charismatic Theology*; Schatzmann, *Pauline Theology of Charismata*.

17. Horton, *What the Bible Says*, 262–63.

18. See Lim, "Spiritual Gifts," 461–62.

19. See Lim, "Spiritual Gifts," 464. The three categories of gifts are teaching and preaching (message of wisdom, message of knowledge); ministry to the church and world (faith, healing, miraculous powers, prophecy, and distinguishing between spirits); and worship (different kind of tongues, interpretation of tongues).

20. See Lim, "Spiritual Gifts," 465–66. "Teaching, seeking divine guidance, counseling, and addressing practical needs in church government and administration may offer

The various lists of spiritual gifts in the NT are not exhaustive[21] but can be divided into enabling gifts and ministry gifts.[22] First Corinthians 12:8–10 lists ministry gifts, while those listed in Eph 4:11 serve as enabling gifts. Enabling gifts "enable persons to set others free for their ministries."[23] The list in 1 Cor 12:28 includes both kinds (the first three listed are enabling, and the last five are ministry). Those who enable others to serve will manifest ministry gifts.[24]

The enabling gifts listed in Eph 4:7–11 are actually spiritually gifted people who are at the same time emphatically Christ's[25] gifts to the church (in contrast to the Spirit's ministry gifts to members of the body in other lists). The pastor-teacher is Christ's gift to the church, gifted by the Spirit to teach.[26]

A Pneumatic versus Secular View of the Teaching-Learning Process

How can Christian educators be certain they are ministering with the Spirit's anointing and not just from natural learned skills? Pneumatic experience in the teaching-learning process provides a necessary corrective to the "schooling instructional model" based on a secularized Western classroom setting that prioritizes cerebral learning.[27] Monte Rice observes that this model has been unconsciously and uncritically adopted by many Asian Christian and Pentecostal educators at the local church and ministerial training levels and ignores most Asians' awareness of and concerns with the spirit world.[28]

Part of the answer to Christian educators' question is to embrace the Pauline view of teaching as a charism of the Spirit. Citing Lim,[29] Rice says that instead of classifying spiritual gifts as natural or supernatural, they

---

occasions for the gift of wisdom" (465).
21. Horton, *What the Bible Says,* 191, 209.
22. Lim, *Spiritual Gifts,* 98–101.
23. Lim, *Spiritual Gifts,* 98.
24. Lim, *Spiritual Gifts,* 98.
25. See Hoehner, "Ephesians," 2:634.
26. Horton, *What the Bible Says,* 269–70; Lim, *Spiritual Gifts,* 106–7, 205.
27. Rice, "Pneumatic Experience."
28. Rice, "Pneumatic Experience," 290–91.
29. Lim, *Spiritual Gifts,* 44–48; Rice, "Pneumatic Experience," 298–300.

should be understood as incarnational and on a continuum between the two poles of natural and supernatural.

Rice agrees with Robert Menzies[30] that the speech gifts (i.e., message of wisdom or knowledge, prophecy, discerning of spirits, tongues and interpretation of tongues) are included in the *pneumatikon* as a subcategory of spiritual gifts. Affirming the position of Robert Clinton and Richard Clinton that word gifts include verbal communication such as prophecy, word of wisdom, word of knowledge, pastoring, evangelism, exhortation, teaching, apostleship and ruling,[31] Rice believes that "the ministerial exercise of the teaching charism as a word-oriented gift should involve a prophetic purpose and dynamic, by virtue of a teacher's experience in Spirit baptism."[32] He cites the support of Lim and of Russell Spittler for the idea that various charisms related to verbal communication are closely associated with teaching ministry.[33]

Summary of the Teaching Gift

The Gospel of Matthew puts a high priority on Jesus's teaching ministry. This ministry was characterized by observable authority and the working of the Spirit. The Great Commission mandates transformative teaching (making disciples). Following the example of Jesus's pneumatic teaching ministry, the apostolic church expected and experienced the dynamic work of the Spirit in the teaching-learning process.

These considerations have significant implications for the training of Spirit-filled local church leaders. Jesus modeled and mandated charismatic, transformative teaching for making disciples. That being the case, how much more must this unambiguous example and requirement be applied in the training of those who will lead congregations today in fulfilling the Great Commission?[34]

30. Menzies, "Spirit-Baptism and Spiritual Gifts," 300.

31. J. Clinton and Clinton, *Developing Leadership Giftedness*, 125–26; Rice, "Pneumatic Experience," 300–303.

32. Rice, "Pneumatic Experience," 302.

33. Lim, *Spiritual Gifts*, 65–74. See Spittler, "Spiritual Gifts"; Rice, "Pneumatic Experience," 300–303; Horton, *What the Bible Says*, 93, 244–48.

34. Conserman, "Assessment of Ministry Formation," 47–51.

PENTECOSTAL/CHARISMATIC DISTINCTIVES IN THE TRAINING PROCESS

The Importance of Training Spirit-Filled Leaders

Ministerial training has historically served as an essential part of the AG's worldwide growth[35] and of many contemporary charismatic movements.[36] As the twenty-first century progresses, these movements must continue to provide training to new generations of leaders. This section will examine the integration of Pentecostal/charismatic distinctives[37] into the delivery and process of ministerial training. The challenge is to offer effective ministerial training that is relevant to its setting and to deliver it in effective ways, while maintaining the movement's pneumatic character.[38]

The Objective of Indigeneity

An important resource for understanding how to facilitate the long-term stability and growth of Christian movements is Melvin Hodges's seminal work *The Indigenous Church*. Hodges served for decades as a missionary in Latin America and as an AG missions leader. He wrote from his experience and observations as a missionary, confirming his understanding of biblical missiology. The objective of missions is "to establish in the country of our labors a strong church patterned after the New Testament example."[39] This process requires proclaiming, gathering believers together for worship and instruction, and selecting and equipping qualified leaders who will continue to provide oversight locally and nationally. The church can then continue to expand, take responsibility for its own leadership and governance,

---

35. McGee, *This Gospel*, 199.

36. See Klaus and Triplett, "National Leadership," 225–26.

37. Essentially, these distinctives can be summed up in the belief that the graces and gifts of the Holy Spirit are available in the contemporary setting. See Burgess et al., *Dictionary of Pentecostal*, 1–5.

38. It should be noted that genuinely Pentecostal and charismatic renewal movements are Christocentric because the Holy Spirit who enlivens them is in his ministry Christocentric.

39. Hodges, *Indigenous Church*, 10.

and provide for its economic needs.[40] Hodges devotes an entire chapter to developing national leadership.[41]

The Spirit and Indigeneity

DeLonn Rance emphasizes Hodges's references to the work of the Spirit in establishing an indigenous national church. He underlines the vital part the Holy Spirit must play in training those called to lead such a movement:

> An indigenous church is a community of believers birthed in a specific context who are Spirit-driven (Spirit-led and Spirit-empowered) to accomplish God's purposes for and through that community. Like the various churches described in the New Testament, particularly in Acts, these local and national communities of faith are to be Spirit-governed, Spirit-supported, and Spirit-propagated. God, by His Spirit, calls and equips local leaders to disciple and mobilize believers in the faith and to guide them in discerning and fulfilling the will of God for their community. The indigenous church is a responsible community that turns to the unlimited resources of the Spirit for its sustenance so as not to depend on the missionary, institutions, ministries, or agencies. It is a community of faith whose members are impassioned and empowered by the Spirit to reach their neighbors, their nation, and their world with the gospel.[42]

An authentically indigenous, Spirit-empowered church must have the means to develop leaders who will continue to guide it along this kind of trajectory. Without this indispensable ingredient in establishing and strengthening the church, an indigenous national church cannot exist.[43] Other logically related aspects of this process that depend on effective training are the multiplication of churches, strong pastoral leadership, and practical application of the principle of the priesthood of all believers.[44]

---

40. Hodges, *Indigenous Church*, 11–12. Hodges's view is that the indigenous national church is to be self-governing, self-propagating, and self-supporting. In recent decades, there has been discussion of variations of this. However, the emphasis in this study is Hodges's view.

41. Hodges, *Indigenous Church*, 53–73. An expected consequence of this process is that the national church will then carry the work into new areas and cultures.

42. Rance, "Fulfilling the Apostolic Mandate," 9–10.

43. Hodges, *Indigenous Church*, 53.

44. See Wagner, "Church Growth Perspective," 274–79.

Training spiritual leaders is as important in Pentecostal missions strategy as focusing on responsive groups and planting indigenous churches among them, mobilizing the entire church to exercise ministry through spiritual gifts, and expecting dynamic demonstrations of spiritual power.[45]

Spirituality and Ministry Education

Although some among Pentecostals and other renewal movements have opposed formal education, there is usually a parallel realization among the movement's leaders of the need for ministerial training. These leaders see a false dichotomy sometimes drawn between spirituality and formal education. Such a view can cause ministers to feel they must choose between spirituality and education. While acknowledging the significant contributions made by self-taught or remarkably gifted individuals, leaders recognize the need to provide quality training for those called into ministry.[46]

Calling for a return to NT methods of ministerial training, Hodges argues that Jesus integrated spiritual growth with increased intellectual understanding and the development of ministry skills.[47] In his view, spirituality and training complement and build upon each other; they are not inconsistent or mutually exclusive.

Integrating Pentecostal/Charismatic Distinctives into Training

While concerns about choosing between spirituality and education can be exaggerated, there is still reason for unease about a lack of balance. Ruthven, while primarily writing about contemporary Pentecostal/charismatic seminary education, echoes some legitimate underlying concerns held by early Pentecostals and others who have spoken against formal ministerial training.[48]

---

45. Pomerville, *Third Force in Missions*, 109.

46. Hollenweger, *Pentecostals*, 472–73.

47. Hodges, *Indigenous Church*, 58–59.

48. Ruthven, *What's Wrong*, 243–68; Conserman, "Assessment of Ministry Formation," 2–4.

Not the Same as Traditional Theological Education

Traditional theological education (TTE) can elevate scholarly learning for its own sake and neglect the development of character and qualifications for spiritual leadership; it values learning by giving titles and recognition that places academic achievers on a pedestal.[49] This kind of training may not produce practitioners who emulate Jesus's and the apostles' ministry; rather, it produces people with higher academic knowledge, who may not value spirituality as much as those who occupy the pews and pulpits of the churches.[50] TTE is sometimes done in a more monastic setting, which creates an artificial barrier between the learning process and the actual ministry situation.[51] In contrast,

> The Biblical model of teaching modalities for Christian workers is characterized by: 1) a significant NT emphasis on the process, 2) implementing a highly-charismatic expression of ministry *skills* or *giftings*, 3) *within settings of actual ministry*, 4) primarily by means of mentoring relationships.[52]

Pneumatic Training as a Corrective

Pentecostal ministerial training can be understood as a corrective to traditional ministerial training, to the extent that traditional training abandoned the convergence of ecclesiology and mission. Traditional training has sometimes been done without a clear understanding that the church is to be the instrument through which God's saving mission in the world is to be accomplished. Alvarez states,

> Mission is not one among many functions of the church, instead the church is a function of God's mission. If the church is the instrument and expression of the Kingdom, then the goal of theological education is to form people in congregations so that they can participate in God's local and global mission.[53]

---

49. Ruthven, *What's Wrong*, 255–59.

50. Ruthven, *What's Wrong*, 258.

51. Ruthven, *What's Wrong*, 263–65.

52. Ruthven, *What's Wrong*, 259–60; italics added.

53. Alvarez, "Distinctives of Pentecostal Education," 286. See Chai, "Pentecostal Theological Education."

He observes further,

> Pentecostal education is not interested in offering purely academic programs. It aims to prepare students mentally, emotionally, spiritually and practically. This means making provision for their personal and spiritual growth, for the development of their ministerial gifts, and for the acquisition of those practical skills they will need in their future life and service.[54]

Alvarez points out four indicators of Pentecostal (and of any genuinely pneumatic) ministerial training: a mentoring orientation, community orientation, emphasis on the priesthood of all believers, and the natural development and exercise of charismata.[55] Mentoring (including equipping all believers for ministry) happens in the context of community. All believers are called to serve and are to do so with the enablement that comes from the Spirit's work in them individually and corporately.

The Pentecostal blending of ecclesiology and mission means that the redemptive effects of the gospel experienced by the individual or believing community are not to be kept at the personal or even the congregational level. Rather, they are to be shared, proclaimed, and passed on to others. This process is to be directed and empowered by the Holy Spirit. In the training process, emerging local church leaders must be formed into spiritual leaders who will perpetuate this way of seeing and doing ministry.

THE HIDDEN CURRICULUM OF THE HOLY SPIRIT

The Responsibility of Educators

Everett McKinney has taught for many decades in Pentecostal training institutions throughout the world. He chronicles his journey as an educator and argues for a continuation of the dynamic, spiritually transforming emphasis characteristic of early Pentecostal schools.[56] The hidden curriculum is the working of the Spirit in students' lives throughout their training experience. To have a Pentecostal education requires educators to be Pentecostal in belief, experience, and practice; but that is insufficient. They must also prove to be deliberate advocates to their students for this way of living and

54. Alvarez, "Distinctives of Pentecostal Education," 286; Conserman, "Assessment of Ministry Formation," 54–57.

55. Alvarez, "Distinctives of Pentecostal Education," 287–89.

56. McKinney, "Some Spiritual Aspects."

doing ministry. This is how leaders maintain the core beliefs, values, and experiences of Pentecostalism and pass them on to the next generation.[57] This is true of any renewal movement's educators and the leadership training process.

The Blending of the Spiritual, Practical, and Academic

Pentecostal and charismatic educators must understand spiritual formation as something that is to happen in tandem with intellectual growth and ministry skills development. As Jesus's disciples experienced, these aspects of ministry training complement and build on each other to form well-rounded ministers.[58] To make these beliefs, philosophy, and experience only part of the formal curriculum is to compartmentalize them.[59] The goal is not just that administrators and instructors have an intellectual grasp of and are in agreement with the reality of the contemporary work of the Spirit; it is that administrators and instructors have internalized those beliefs, experiences, and values, so they instinctively teach and model them.[60] Blending of the academic, spiritual, and practical must be intentional.[61] For those entrusted with training the next generation of Spirit-filled local church leaders, the exercise of formulating a personal philosophy of Pentecostal or charismatic education can be an expression of this intentionality and a helpful first step.[62]

Summary of Pneumatic Distinctives in the Training Process

Effective, relevant training for spiritual leaders is not an option. To form Spirit-filled local church leaders, the Holy Spirit must be intimately involved in every facet of the training process. Every aspect of training must be considered a space for the Spirit to work without hindrance in the lives of emerging leaders.

57. McKinney, "Some Spiritual Aspects," 254.

58. Hodges, *Indigenous Church*, 59.

59. McKinney, "Some Spiritual Aspects," 260.

60. McKinney, "Some Spiritual Aspects," 260.

61. Such a blended, holistic means of training is the only way to ensure that those who train ministers can impart these values to their students, facilitating the formation of holistically equipped spiritual leaders.

62. McKinney, "Some Spiritual Aspects," 263.

CONCLUSION

This chapter addresses what I believe is the heart of what is needed in the training of Spirit-filled local church leaders for the twenty-first century. The secular Western schooling instructional model is a poor substitute for the dynamic, anointed, transformational kind of teaching that Jesus demonstrated and commissioned the church to continue in perpetuity. Genuine Christian teaching, no matter at what level—CE or children's ministry within the physical walls of a church building, small groups in a home, neighborhood outreach ministry in a public setting, or a ministry training program—must be an adventure, in which lives are transformed through the present, dynamic working of the Holy Spirit. If our teaching is not transformational, let us not call it Christian teaching.

Chapter 8

Demographic Expansion of Training

INTRODUCTION

RENEWAL MOVEMENTS HAVE A heritage of inclusiveness—racial, gender, age, and socioeconomic status. Although church historians have documented ways in which such movements have sometimes struggled and failed to live up to that ideal,[1] such movements have still demonstrated a willingness to strive for it. This chapter looks at theological issues that have practical implications for the availability of Spirit-filled ministerial training. It then discusses those implications and gives recommendations for training based on those issues and factors.

THEOLOGICAL ISSUES

The Promise of the Universal Outpouring of the Spirit: Old Testament

The OT has at least two notable passages that foreshadow the NT fulfillment that was intended to characterize the NT church throughout its history. This promise began to be fulfilled at Pentecost and has gained unprecedented traction worldwide through the various waves of the outpouring

---

1. Newman, *Race and the Assemblies*; see also Cox, *Fire from Heaven*, 58–64; Everts Powers, "Your Daughters Shall Prophesy," 321–22; Gill and Cavaness, *God's Women*.

of the Holy Spirit that began to take place in the decades leading up to the beginning of the twentieth century.[2]

Numbers 11:24–30

Moses's remarkable exclamation in Num 11:29, "Would that all the Lord's people were prophets, that the Lord would put His Spirit upon them!" comes out of his experience of God's provision for an overwhelming need. In the midst of a leadership crisis among the Hebrews (Num 11:10–30), Moses is overworked and emotionally unable to carry the responsibility by himself. God instructs Moses to select seventy recognized elders to assist him. When they gather together, God distributes the Spirit on the elders chosen to assist Moses in providing spiritual and civil oversight to the nation.[3]

As a result of this unusual (for that time) impartation of the Spirit, the group of elders prophesies. After the others cease and depart, two of the seventy, Eldad and Medad, remain and continue to prophesy. When Moses's assistant Joshua questions him about this, Moses's words reflect what Roger Stronstad sees as a heartfelt desire that was fulfilled at Pentecost.[4]

This distribution of the Spirit is a case of encounter with and mission through the Spirit spreading among an expanding number of people.

Joel 2:28–32

This passage has a number of remarkable references to the universal nature of the promise of the Spirit. The first is the promise to pour out the Spirit abundantly like a rain shower in quantity and quality (v. 28a), in contrast to how the Spirit had been experienced before.[5] Although the receivers of this outpouring are called "all flesh" or "all mankind," it is clear that in the

---

2. Synan, *Century of the Holy Spirit*, 1–13. For the historical background of the twentieth-century pneumatic renewal movements, see Synan, *Holiness-Pentecostal Movement*; Dayton, *Theological Roots of Pentecostalism*.

3. See Whitelaw, *Numbers*, 109–11.

4. Stronstad, *Charismatic Theology*, 58–59. See Stronstad, "Prophethood of All Believers," 61–62.

5. See Given, *Joel*, 27–28. Given ties this in with the NT theme of inclusion of Gal 3:28, "neither Greek nor Jew, circumcision nor uncircumcision, barbarian, Scythian, bond nor free; but Christ is all, and in all."

writer's and the readers' minds, the reference is limited to those included in the nation of Israel (see v. 32). At the same time, there is an important image of expansion. This expansion now extended beyond those segments who had previously been seen as potentially pneumatic (prophets, priests, sages, and kings, the official and unofficial leadership class) to all in Zion.

Second, the promise of the Spirit is given to the various members of general Israelite society (v. 28b; sons, daughters, old men, and young men). This gives additional specificity to the fulfillment of Moses's desire in Num 11:29 that all God's people would be prophets and would experience the Spirit working in and through them.[6]

Third, Joel predicts that even more (v. 29a) than on those mentioned before, the Spirit will be poured out on society's non-members—slaves—than on those counted as members of the society.[7] He also gives a universal call for deliverance in verse 32: "Whoever calls on the name of the Lord will be delivered." However, it must be noted that this call is in specific reference to the Jewish survivors on Mount Zion and in Jerusalem.

The Fulfillment of the Promise: New Testament (Acts 2:16–21)

Joel 2 is the starting point of Peter's Pentecost sermon. While Joel speaks in universal terms about the offer of deliverance specifically to those in Mount Zion and Jerusalem, Peter's Pentecost sermon[8] broadens the scope even more, providing a "democratization of the Spirit."[9] It is likely that in retrospect, Luke saw the foreshadowing of the universal outreach to the gentiles, but that Peter did not understand it at the time.[10] While both Joel and Peter did not yet recognize it,

> the abundant outpouring of the Spirit is thus available for all, Jew or Gentile, rich or poor, young or old, educated or uneducated, regardless of race, color, or national origin. Nor would this out-pouring be a one-time event. The Hebrew indicates progressive or repeated action, making the outpouring of the Spirit available to

---

6. See L. Allen, "Joel," 789.

7. See Given, *Joel*, 28.

8. Although there are notable differences in Joel's prophecy and Peter's citation of it, only those aspects relevant to demographics will be noted here.

9. Lidbeck, *Resurrection and Spirit*, 203.

10. F. Bruce, *Book of Acts*, 68.

generation after generation. It can, of course, be rejected or disregarded, but it remains available.[11]

It is especially striking that in Acts 2:21, Peter left out the phrase "Mount Zion and Jerusalem," in contrast to Joel 2:32, "For on Mount Zion and in Jerusalem there will be those who escape, as the Lord has said, even among the survivors whom the Lord calls." Although Joel's prophecy dealt with Israel, Peter applied the prophecy about the outpouring of the Spirit to the church:

> Such an announcement would seem incredible to the Jews, because they thought God's Spirit was given only to a few select people (see Num. 11:28–29). But here were 120 of their fellow Jews, men and women, enjoying the blessing of the same Holy Spirit that had empowered Moses, David, and the prophets.[12]

In referring to the church, Peter broadens the scope even further by ennobling Joel's inclusive view of slaves or bondservants (v. 18). Rather than identifying these chattel human possessions as simple servants or slaves without any legal standing, they are "my [God's] bond slaves, both men and women."[13]

At Pentecost, the universal call to repentance and salvation, along with the offer of the experience of the Spirit that qualifies for mission and service (that had previously been by default directed toward the Israelites and their leadership class) was directed toward a radically different audience. That call was now truly universal, encompassing all of humankind. This concept was so new, so unheard of, and so revolutionary in the minds of Peter's hearers that it would forever change Judaism, the seedbed of the church. As this call went forward in the church, it would also change forever the surrounding gentile world.

Inclusion Themes in Scripture (Galatians 3:22–29)

An emphasis in the NT[14] (compare Rom 10:11–13; 1 Cor 12:12–13; Col 3:10–11) that undergirds demographic expansion is the inclusive nature

11. Horton, *What the Bible Says*, 57.

12. Wiersbe, *Bible Exposition Commentary*, 1:409.

13. Lidbeck, *Resurrection and Spirit*, 168.

14. The OT also intimates inclusion themes, although not in as overt ways as the NT. Some of these expressions are in the stories of Rahab (Josh 2 and 6) and the book of Ruth

of the gospel and its application in the lives of those who experience its reality and transformative power. While incorporation into Christ does not change someone's gender, socioeconomic, or ethnic status, "it does mean that these things are of no value or handicap when it comes to our spiritual relationship to God through Christ."[15]

The first aspect of universality is negative. All who are outside of Christ, regardless of status, are spiritually lost (Gal 3:22). A new people[16] made up of those who believe in Christ, regardless of gender, ethnicity, or socioeconomic status, has been constituted (v. 23).[17] Because racism, sexism, and socioeconomic discrimination have been manifest symptoms of humanity's fallen condition throughout history, this is a profound and important aspect of the gospel.

It is important to view the inclusiveness of the gospel in the context of first-century culture.[18] The tendency of some today is to compare the advances in society's treatment of the various demographics discussed here from a twenty-first-century perspective rather than from a first-century one. One reason to avoid this error is that viewing from today's perspective blinds us to the radical nature of gospel inclusiveness in regard to gender,[19] ethnicity, race, age, and socioeconomic status.

---

and their inclusion in the lineage of Christ (Matt 1:5); see also the healing of Naaman (2 Kgs 5:1–14). Provision was also made for foreigners living among the Jews to assimilate and be converted (Exod 12:48–49).

15. Wiersbe, *Bible Exposition Commentary,* 1:704.

16. Fee, *Paul, the Spirit,* 63–73.

17. Wuest, *Wuest's Word Studies,* 3:112; Robertson, "Gal 3:28," in *Word Pictures.* Wuest says, "The individual differences between Jew and Greek, between slave and free, between male and female, are merged in that higher unity into which all believers are raised by the fact that they all have a common life in Christ Jesus. One heart now beats in all. The pulsating life of the Lord Jesus is the motive power. One mind guides all, the mind of Christ. One life is lived by all, the life of the Lord Jesus produced by the Holy Spirit in the various circumstances and relations of each individual believer's experience."

18. Lohse, *New Testament Environment,* 146–50, 208–16.

19. One reality of the early twenty-first century is that there is a plethora of gender related theologies that have developed during the preceding decades. My perspective on gender reflects the traditional biblical view of human sexuality.

Gender

Sons (*uioi*, Gal 3:26), although masculine, is a generic term for male and female children.[20] Jamieson et al. believe that "neither male nor female" (v. 28) may be more accurately rendered "there is not male and female." They go on to say,

> There is no distinction into male and female. Difference of sex makes no difference in Christian privileges. But under the law the male sex had great privileges. Males alone had in their body circumcision, the sign of the covenant (contrast *baptism* applied to male and female alike); they alone were capable of being kings and priests, whereas all of either sex are now "kings and priests unto God" (Rev 1:6); they had prior right to inheritances.[21]

The negative universality of Gal 3:22 that confines all humans under the condemnation of sin regardless of gender is not limited by the individual's gender and does not change one's gender. In the same way, the positive inclusiveness of the gospel is not limited by gender and does not change one's gender.

It might be asked why Jesus did not include women in the group of his called apostles. The obvious answer seems to be that to do so would have created enough cultural tension to sidetrack him from fulfilling the ultimate salvific purposes for his ministry. At the same time, the evangelists allude to how Jesus and the Twelve were accompanied by a group of women who were involved with his ministry in practical ways that were supportive (Matt 27:55–56; Luke 8:1–3; 10:38–42).[22] By selecting various members of the Twelve from different socioeconomic demographics and political persuasions, it is evident that Jesus exercised inclusion, but not of the kind that would be self-defeating in the social milieu in which he ministered.

Paul recognized and affirmed the validity of women in ministry. In Rom 16, he lists a number of his fellow ministers, many of whom are women. Some of the women who ministered with him or whose ministries were known and affirmed by him were Euodia and Syntyche in Philippi, the daughters of Philip the evangelist, and Tryphena and Tryphosa in Rome.[23]

---

20. Robertson, "Gal 3:26," in *Word Pictures*.

21. Jamieson et al, *Commentary Critical*, 2:332. See Everts Powers, "Your Daughters Shall Prophesy"; Kowalski, "Role of Women in Ministry."

22. McGill and Cavaness, *God's Women*, 73–82.

23. Kowalski, "Role of Women in Ministry." See also Lumahan, "Facts and Figures,"

Ethnicity

Paul changes from *we* (Gal 3:23–25) to *you* (vv. 26–29). In making this switch from first person (Jews) to second person (his readers, both Jewish and gentile), he demonstrates that Christ's cross has destroyed the barrier between the two groups and that all members of the two groups who are in Christ are now co-equal in their relationship with God.[24]

One instance in Jesus's ministry that has sometimes been misunderstood is his encounter with the Syrophoenician woman and her young, demonized daughter (Matt 15:22–28; Mark 7:24–30). The evangelists describe Jesus as ignoring her at first and finally responding to her in a way that would seem racist by today's standards. However, both evangelists stress her faith and persistence in interceding on behalf of her daughter. They also mention her acknowledgment that she understood that, as gentiles, she and her daughter were unworthy to receive blessings from a Jewish rabbi. Regardless, Jesus responded positively to her faith and perseverance and granted her request for mercy.

Two other observations may serve to clarify any confusion about this episode. First, Jesus attributed his response to the humility and faith that the mother expressed. She and the disciples appear to be the ones who saw race as an issue here, not Jesus. Second, Jesus's reference to being sent to the lost sheep of the house of Israel (a remark recorded only by Matthew) may have been more of a reference to strategy than to any relative value that he attributed to ethnic groups.

Socioeconomic Status

Paul mentions the slave before the free (Gal 3:28).[25] Although some have mistakenly implied or taught that God actually favors the poor over other socioeconomic groups,[26] it is clear that the gospel addressed socioeconomic

---

74–77. Lumahan describes the revivalist milieu and early Pentecostal hermeneutic that allowed and encouraged women's involvement in ministry and leadership. This was a powerful influence on the AG pioneers in Southern Ilocos, and he credits many female spiritual leaders for the advance of the AG in that area. This is characteristic of many renewal movements.

24. Wuest, *Word Studies*, 3:111; Mathews and Park, *Post-Racial Church*.

25. Jamieson et al., *Commentary Critical*, 2:332.

26. Nash, *Poverty and Wealth*, 106.

divisions in the first century in ways that were revolutionary,[27] and that it continues to do so.

In addition to its many commands to treat the poor with justice, the OT makes allowances for the poor to participate in worship (Lev 14:21–32). In this passage, those without the means to provide the prescribed amount and kind of sacrifices could substitute others and offer smaller amounts. It also prescribes equal treatment of all socioeconomic classes: "You shall do no injustice in judgment; you shall not be partial to the poor nor defer to the great, but you are to judge your neighbor fairly" (Lev 19:15). The Gospels make it clear that Jesus practiced the OT priority of benevolence and justice to the poor.

A brief survey of the Gospel of Matthew, noting Jesus's interactions with and reactions to people at various socioeconomic levels, is revealing. Matthew 6:19–34 contrasts what can be besetting sins, related to wealth, of the rich and poor. The rich may prioritize their riches, and the poor may not trust God for their needs. In 8:5–13, Jesus commends the faith of the Roman centurion who was in a position of privilege and power. In 9:9, he calls a wealthy tax gatherer to follow him. In 9:20–22, he commends the faith of a woman with an issue of blood, someone who is at the very bottom of the social spectrum. In 9:27–30, he commends the faith of two blind men, who were also nearly at the bottom of the spectrum. In 9:36, he feels compassion for the multitudes who had little power or influence. In 11:25–30, he calls the oppressed multitudes to respond to his appeal for rest. In 13:23, the cares of life and riches choke the word; this reality requires the disciple to persevere in faith. In 16:24–26, he issues a challenge to all disciples, regardless of socioeconomic status, to faith and sacrifice in light of their accountability to God. Matthew 19:16–26 is a call to obedience; the issue is not riches but willingness to obey.

For Jesus, the bottom line was not where an individual or group of people happened to be on the socioeconomic spectrum. There was no virtue in poverty or powerlessness, nor was there a greater likelihood that an individual would not be saved specifically because he was tainted by wealth or power. Jesus commended faith and obedience and condemned unbelief and disobedience, regardless of the individual's socioeconomic position.

---

27. Keener, "Gal 3:28," in *IVP Bible Background Commentary*.

Age

One of the areas that Judaism and Christianity have revolutionized throughout history is the social status of children. While the Israelites did not consistently recognize or live out this truth, it is clearly enunciated in the OT. God places value on the young: parents are to teach God's words to their children (Deut 6:4–7); children are to be considered a blessing from the Lord (Ps 127:3–5).

Jesus, in his words and manner of relating to children, raised the bar further. Certain aspects of children's behavior are to be emulated, and great punishment awaits those who abuse them (Matt 18:1–6). They are to be blessed and encouraged in spiritual things (19:13–15).

On the other end of the age spectrum, the elderly are given a special status in Scripture. They are to be given respect and honor as an expression of reverence for God (Lev 19:32; Prov 23:22). They are to be considered a source of wisdom, including their knowledge of the past (Deut 32:7). They are also promised continued productiveness in their golden years (Ps 92:14).

The value that Scripture places on elders and the young is reflected in Joel's prophecy and in Peter's preaching at Pentecost. These observations indicate that age *per se* does not affect the entitlement of a believer to be involved in God's work and thus to receive whatever training is needed for that. Abilities, passions, and so on will change with each stage of an individual believer's life. However, God's desire that he or she experience encounter, empowerment, and mission remains constant.

IMPLICATIONS FOR SPIRIT-FILLED MINISTERIAL TRAINING

Teaching

It is probable that many at all levels of a renewal movement agree in theory with the idea of including all age groups as potential students. However, in reality, this ideal may remain beyond the will or means to do what is required to move training opportunities in this direction. To find the potential for real-world expression, this positive sentiment about accommodating various demographics must be connected to and motivated by the topic of this chapter, the theological concept of a universal outpouring of

the Spirit that will reach all people.[28] All stakeholders of ministerial training need to stay aware and convinced of the theological necessity of doing
this; only then will they be motivated to seek practical ways to make this
happen.[29]

Denominational leaders must first clearly communicate this connection to local church leaders. Denominational functions provide one setting for this communication. Another setting is the teaching that students
receive in their ministerial training courses.

However, communicating this connection in such settings serves only
as a preliminary step. It must ultimately become understood and embraced
at the grassroots level. People in the local churches must see it practically
demonstrated in the lives of their leaders and hear it expounded in preaching and teaching. Over time, church members will take ownership of this
idea.

Student Recruitment

Delivery of training begins with recruitment of students.[30] At first glance,
this may seem a practical issue or one of deference and respect to the various demographic groups. However, one should see it first as a theological
issue, because the universality of the promise of the outpouring of the
Spirit is a core ingredient of Pentecostalism and other pneumatic renewal
movements.[31]

Stakeholders and grassroots members must understand this connection. Only then will broad recruitment for ministry training have deep and
widespread support from the church constituency.

28. See Stronstad, "Prophethood of All Believers," 60–77.

29. Banks, *Reenvisioning Theological Education*, 122.

30. Recruitment should be seen in much broader terms than just going to churches
or youth events and inviting young people to attend Bible school. I have observed the
effectiveness of this strategy, but it sometimes appears to lack the purposeful, intentional
process of cooperation between the church and the school that provides a way to prepare
students who sense a call to ministry and who demonstrate the willingness and ability
to prepare for it.

31. Stronstad, *Charismatic Theology*, 25–26, 56–58.

Training Infrastructure

Educators must recognize the diverse demographics that make up the body of potential students for ministerial training. They need to think in terms of an infrastructure that can accommodate many demographics,[32] rather than in terms of an individual institution or training delivery system that could easily miss significant demographic blocs of potential students.

CONCLUSION

One characteristic of Generation Z (at least in the West) is that they are much more comfortable with demographic diversity than earlier generations were.[33] This bodes well for the theme of this chapter about broadening the demographic reach of training institutions in the coming decades of the twenty-first century.

This chapter demonstrates a clear pattern of the ever-expanding availability of the Spirit in fulfillment of God's expressed desire, beginning in the OT and continuing throughout the NT. The expansion involved numbers of people and an increasing variety of demographic groups. The experience of the Spirit takes the form of encounter, incorporation/inclusion, equipment and empowerment, and involvement in mission.

Those who today are in Christ are now God's people first and foremost, regardless of any demographic characteristics. If this is true of the universal church, it will also reflect those who are called to lead the local church. Training opportunities for God-called, Spirit-filled leaders should then be offered to a broadening number of people and demographic groups.

Scripture reflects God's inclusive attitude toward all demographic groups. This inclusiveness should characterize the availability of training. The accessibility of training opportunities should be conditioned not by preferring or disallowing certain demographics, but by the potential individual students' ability to meet the qualifications in Scripture and of educators and denominational leadership, regardless of demographics.

32. See ch. 9 of this book, "Training Infrastructure."
33. Barna Group, *Gen Z*, 105–6.

Chapter 9

Training Infrastructure

INTRODUCTION

When thinking of ministerial training, the tendency is to think of one institution or platform for delivering training: a residential Bible school or seminary that is part of a university, a correspondence school like Global University, or a short-term intensive school like Masters Commission (MC). This chapter advocates for changing the paradigm of how Spirit-filled ministerial and local church leadership training are offered by expanding options made available to potential students. The paradigm should be changed from a one-platform delivery system to a training infrastructure.

CHALLENGES FACED BY MANY TRAINING INSTITUTIONS

A number of problems and challenges face those involved with ministerial education. Changing how training is organized and carried out can provide solutions for some of these challenges.

One problem is that those who desire training represent a variety of demographic backgrounds. This variety can involve age or marital and family status; work, career, or educational background; and location. All of these variables and characteristics affect the ability of potential students to access training opportunities and successfully complete training courses.

Another challenge is that ministry training schools are often not structured to serve more than a portion of the people who desire to study for ministry and who come from various demographic groups represented in the churches. Many training institutions realize this but are unable to innovate enough to reach underserved demographic groups. For example, if academic requirements are given too much weight in the admissions process, potential students who are weak academically—but otherwise qualified for leadership because of their spiritual maturity, Christlike character, sense of calling, and recommendation from their home church—could miss out on the training offered.[1]

A third problem is that new training schools, established by well-intended entrepreneurs, sometimes experience unintended negative results. Those results can entail redundancy or overlap of training programs and even unhealthy competition between schools that appeal to a similar demographic of potential students. This can lead to unnecessarily stretching limited resources (human, economic, and facilities) and overlooking or neglecting underserved demographics. The underlying issue is theological. The availability of training opportunities must reflect the ideal discussed in chapter 8 of this book, "Demographic Expansion of Training."

The Need for Innovation in Training

The one key to long-term local and national church growth may be effective leadership training.[2] Byron Klaus and Loren Triplett discuss how to ensure that Pentecostal training institutions will continue to successfully fulfill this specific vital purpose. They emphasize that Pentecostals have historically been innovative in maintaining effective and relevant training programs.[3] Ministerial training that develops leaders who can multiply themselves must continue to innovate in the face of the massive changes taking place, without that training losing its characteristic dependence on the Holy Spirit. To do this requires providing as many training alternatives as possible.[4]

1. Young, "Planning Theological Education," 74; Banks, *Reenvisioning Theological Education*, 194–95.

2. M. Williams, *Partnership in Mission*, 124.

3. See Klaus and Triplett, "National Leadership," 234–37.

4. M. Williams, *Partnership in Mission*, 124–47. Williams, writing in the 1970s primarily from the perspective of ministry in Africa, mentions self-study, apprenticeships,

The lack of a pronounced clergy-laity distinction, especially in early generations, made the training of members as lay ministers a natural part of Pentecostal leadership development.[5] Some observers of Pentecostal ministerial training have seen non-formal or informal in-service training as even more effective and efficient.[6] Although too much of a distinction can be made between formal and informal or non-formal education,[7] simply maintaining a particular model or style of training must never take precedence over the real goal: forming genuinely Spirit-filled local church leaders.[8] Those who provide training must stay open to ways of improving that training and broadening accessibility. Informal and non-formal training are more accessible to local congregations than a Bible institute, and these give opportunity to those gifted for congregational leadership beyond evangelism and small groups to move to higher levels of leadership.[9]

The Bible Institute Model

Many twentieth-century ministerial training programs worldwide were patterned on the European theological college[10] and the North American Bible institute models.[11] Early Pentecostal missionaries used the Bible institute model, which incorporated the same "intense biblical education, dynamic spiritual atmosphere, and quicker movement into actual ministry" that they had experienced in their own training. This has been effective, especially when combined with high spiritual fervor.[12]

The Bible institute model has proven an efficient way to prepare large numbers of leaders and has varied in duration and type of facilities used. It

and traditional residential Bible schools. In the intervening decades, a number of other possible models have arisen, such as church-based part-time training. In addition, advances in technology have increased the potential for variety in training platforms.

5. See Klaus and Triplett, "National Leadership," 226.

6. See Klaus and Triplett, "National Leadership," 228–29.

7. Hodkinson et al, "Interrelationships."

8. Hodges, *Indigenous Church*, 65.

9. See Klaus and Triplett, "National Leadership," 228–29. It should be noted that those best served by informal and non-formal training might include people who do not fit into traditional academic standards.

10. Rowdon, "Theological Education," 83–85.

11. See Klaus and Triplett, "National Leadership," 227; Brereton, *Training God's Army*; ch. 11 of this book, "Leadership Development in Church History."

12. See Klaus and Triplett, "National Leadership," 227.

has often incorporated practical ministry experience as part of the course of study.[13] While many have recognized the vital part that the development of emerging leaders has played in the expansion of the Pentecostal/charismatic movement worldwide, the continued success of this particular model for today should not be presumed upon.[14]

Pentecostals and other renewal movements have demonstrated the ability to adapt to changing conditions and devise new ways to provide training. Some methods that have proven effective are correspondence and distance education and short-term intensive continuing education opportunities for ministers.[15] Klaus and Triplett challenge Pentecostal educators:

> While the need of leadership for younger churches is important, there exists an even more strategic question for Pentecostals. Simply stated, how do they form leaders adequately and yet keep the Pentecostal missionary spirit alive to carry out the mandate of global evangelization? With such an agenda facing Pentecostals, it must be acknowledged that educational structures and processes, in addition to the content, of course, work together in the formation of leadership.[16]

This innovative spirit continues to be vital today. The bottom-line question is: how can educators update existing training delivery systems and create new ones that can provide local church leaders in sufficient quality and numbers to guide the present-day church in fulfilling the Great Commission?

THE TRAINING INFRASTRUCTURE

Instead of thinking in terms of one school or one way of delivering training (or even two) as an entity in itself, an infrastructure system of training can be established.[17] A training infrastructure consists of multiple styles and kinds of training and means of delivering it, based on student availability, anticipated or current type and location of ministry, academic

---

13. See Klaus and Triplett, "National Leadership," 227.

14. See Klaus and Triplett, "National Leadership," 233; Elliston, *Home Grown Leaders*, 75–76.

15. See Klaus and Triplett, "National Leadership," 229–30.

16. See Klaus and Triplett, "National Leadership," 231–32.

17. Some synonyms for infrastructure are configuration, edifice, frame, framework, shell, skeleton, and structure.

considerations, and so on.[18] There are also multiple levels of training, based on the level or kind of training needed by a group of students at a given time. Training takes the form of an infrastructure that consists of various parts. Each part serves a different group of students with different needs, characteristics, or availability.

Elliston describes five generalized levels or types of leadership needed by the church that reflect the NT teaching on the gifting of the Spirit.[19] Each type of leader is essential in the fulfillment of the Great Commission, and each type needs its own specialized kind of training.

Briefly, Level 1 leaders are volunteers who through their teaching or serving ministry directly touch the lives of a small group of people (normally up to twenty) in their local congregation. Little specialized or formal training is required for their ministry. They are the most numerous kinds of leaders and particularly vital in serving the needs of new believers and the numeric growth and overall health of the congregation.

Level 2 leaders are also volunteers, usually with more training and experience in ministry than Level 1, and whose area of ministry or leadership has a broader reach of indirect influence and spiritual care. They may oversee the ministry of those in teaching or other ministries, or they may serve in leadership positions in the congregation. They often work closely with pastoral leadership and represent that leadership to the congregation.

Level 3 leaders are often pastors of small congregations, and their direct or indirect influence includes the entire congregation and ideally the surrounding community beyond the walls of the church. They usually have official ministerial credentials or are working toward acquiring them.

Level 4 leaders are pastors of larger congregations, and their direct influence is often with other staff who assist them in providing pastoral leadership. This type of leader also includes directors of parachurch ministries. They have a proven ministry and have probably completed some level of formal training. Their direct and indirect influence extends throughout the town or city where they pastor and may even reach beyond their local area.

Level 5 leaders may be in denominational leadership, education, writing ministry, or other positions from which they influence masses of people indirectly. However, their direct influence on individuals is no broader than

18. Banks, *Reenvisioning Theological Education*, 191–97.

19. Elliston, *Home Grown Leaders*, 26–35. Elliston is careful to explain that in describing these types of leaders in this way, he is not advocating a non-biblical hierarchy in church leadership or implying that some types of leaders/leadership are less valuable than others.

those at other levels of leadership (up to twenty). These leaders tend to have the highest level of formal education but should be continually sharpened through their interactions with various individuals and groups with whom they come into contact.

Carl Gibbs provides a somewhat similar view of training based on the various levels of training needed and the specific purpose of each level.[20] He lists five levels of training, each targeting a specific group of believers based on their current or anticipated role. This arrangement can be described as a training pyramid, where each level provides a foundation for the next one. The levels of the training pyramid are disciples (all); lay leaders (one to twelve ratio, similar to Levels 1 and 2); bi-vocational leaders of small groups and emerging congregations (one to thirty or forty ratio, similar to Level 3); full-time leaders (one to sixty ratio, similar to Level 4), and scholars (one to 1000 ratio, similar to Level 5).

The middle three levels of the training pyramid (lay leaders, bi-vocational leaders, and full-time leaders) should be the primary shared concern of the local church, training institution, and denominational leadership.[21] Each level should combine practical and appropriate academic learning and skills development, along with spiritual formation. Each step toward a higher level of spiritual responsibility should lead to an increase in the challenge and intensity of the training.

A pyramid training structure is a means to a desired outcome. The variety of levels in training is provided so that local churches can advance God's redemptive purpose in the world. The aim of training is to establish and maintain congregations that are genuinely spiritual and effective in evangelism and disciple making. To do this, the training must train lay and full-time leaders who can make disciples, provide pastoral care, establish newly planted congregations, and prepare denominational leaders to effectively oversee the movements they serve.[22]

Derek Tan advocates for providing training opportunities for church members not called to full-time ministry while continuing to provide training for those who are called to full-time ministry:

20. Gibbs, "Training Pyramid," 103–32.

21. Gibbs, "Training Pyramid," 111–17. However, the infrastructure should work with the local church in the training of lay leaders. This provides another excellent opportunity to foster a cooperative relationship between the two entities. Leaders working toward an advanced degree can ideally do so at a seminary that is under the authority of or working in partnership with denominational leadership.

22. Hodges, *Indigenous Church*, 53–54, 61–62, 69–70.

While there is still a dire need to train more clergy for the growing church, there is a neglect of the needs of equipping the laity of the community of faith. In today's church, a large slice of the ministry is carried by the laity and they need to be equipped. Institutions that have a "full-time calling" tag for admission portray themselves as elitist clubs and catering to the selected few and not the whole.[23]

The paradigm of what a training institution looks like must be changed from an individual school or delivery model to an infrastructure made up of various interrelated parts that is flexible enough to adapt to changing conditions and needs. Four things should characterize this infrastructure:

1. Ability to provide multiple levels of training;

2. Accessibility to as many demographic groups as possible (age, marital and family status, work background, location, and academic background);

3. Shared sense of ownership between educators and all stakeholders, such as denominational leadership and local churches;

4. Integration into the operation and discipleship training activities of local congregations.

BENEFITS OF A TRAINING INFRASTRUCTURE

Several benefits derive from embracing and setting up a training infra-structure like this. First, it provides tangible affirmation to the theological value of the universal outpouring of the Holy Spirit.[24] Second, it provides a response to the negatives of upward lift, such as clergy professionalization and clergy-laity divide, which can strongly inhibit the ongoing effectiveness of churches in fulfilling the Great Commission. Third, it promotes the con-cept of ongoing training for every level of believer. Fourth, it strengthens the organic connection between the church and the training institution and maintains a holistic balance in the training process and content. The next few paragraphs expand on some of these benefits.

---

23. See Tan, "Theological Education in Asia," 89.

24. See ch. 8 of this book, "Demographic Expansion of Training."

It Addresses Upward Lift

Upward lift or *redemption and lift* refers to economic and social advances experienced by individual believers and congregations coming from a lower socioeconomic status.[25] These believers and congregations experience such advances as a direct or indirect result of their experience of the gospel. Klaus and Triplett ask what can be done about the aspects of upward lift that can interfere with the processes that lead to church multiplication and continued aggressive evangelism and discipleship. Upward lift can result in ministerial professionalization, decreased dependence on the Spirit, routinization, and slowdown of church growth. Focusing on smaller numbers of specialized students rather than equipping all who want to serve can negatively affect long-term growth and expansion.[26]

It Provides for Ongoing Training

Today, spiritual leaders often need additional training or advanced degrees.[27] A training infrastructure such as the one described above can provide this, while simultaneously offering church members and workers, especially those in Levels 1–3 leadership, who desire to serve the opportunities to be trained and equipped for service. This ability depends on the leaders of the infrastructure remaining sensitive to the guidance of the Spirit and the needs of their constituency.

It Maintains Balance in Training

Maintenance of the holistic character of Pentecostal ministerial training remains extremely important. Such training must not fall into the imbalances for which it became a corrective.[28] If imbalance does occur (in forms such as upward lift, leading to professionalization and unhealthy specialization in ministry, and the narrowing of training opportunities for Level 1–3 workers), Pentecostalism and other renewal movements will lose their identity. Mission stands as the one singular task of the church; out of this one mandate, all else must flow. The church's structure, leadership,

25. Wagner, *Spiritual Power*, 68–70, 87–88.
26. See Klaus and Triplett, "National Leadership," 231–35.
27. See Klaus and Triplett, "National Leadership," 237.
28. Alvarez, "Distinctives of Pentecostal Education," 281–93.

mobilization, and training exist for the specific purpose of carrying out the Great Commission locally and throughout the world.

It Provides a Bridge between Formal, Non-Formal, and Informal Training

Ted Ward and Samuel Rowen popularized the concept of the rail-fence analogy several decades ago.[29] This analogy is a way of explaining how the various educational formats or settings (formal, non-formal, and informal) can build upon and complement each other's contribution to the teaching-learning process. The rail-fence analogy combines the cognitive/theoretical content that characterizes much of formal education with the actual experience and reality of doing ministry. It does this by providing periodic opportunities[30] to discuss and process together from the various experiences and settings of learning and ministry.[31]

CONCLUSION

There are a number of considerations that call for educators to innovate. These considerations include changing conditions throughout the world, diverse demographics who want and need ministry training, the varieties of training needed, and the reality that various demographics may be underserved. The creation and maintenance of a training infrastructure can make possible many of the innovations that are and will be needed as the twenty-first century moves forward.

It is self-evident that facilitating and participating in a paradigmatic change as described in this chapter is not a convenient or comfortable proposition. The practical aspects of how it can be done are daunting enough, without even considering the required change in how educators and other stockholders think about ministry training.

---

29. Ward and Rowen, "Rail-Fence Analogy," 47–51.

30. Ward and Rowen call them seminars for lack of a more appropriate term; I would characterize them as debriefings.

31. One caveat: Ward and Rowen emphasize what appears to be a cognitive, skill, scientific method/approach to the professional aspects of ministry training (the Berlin model). Educators need to put a conscious and intentional emphasis on what Rowen identifies as the *being* aspect of training, which is dependent on the hidden curriculum of the Holy Spirit (Ward and Rowen, "Rail-Fence Analogy," 47–48).

Reimagining and creating a new paradigm of ministry training may in some ways resemble the difficult process in which the formulation of the university model of education took place.[32] However, the foundational worldview of renewal educators is (or should be) entirely different from that of the Enlightenment worldview that motivated the establishment of the university model and in many ways, for centuries, negatively affected the trajectory of theological education.[33] The motivation behind making this transition is that it has the potential of changing ministerial training in an equally profound way for the future. But this change promises to be a much more positive one.

32. See ch. 11 of this book, "Leadership Development in Church History."
33. González, *History of Theological Education*, 107; Ruthven, *What's Wrong*, 1–4.

Chapter 10

Mentoring

INTRODUCTION

NOTHING IN THE DISCIPLES' training experience could replace just being with Jesus (Mark 3:14). Training by association,[1] the intentional practice of instructors spending time with their students, is an invaluable part of what those involved with ministerial training can do to form students into effective spiritual leaders. Some of the most profound conversations between Jesus and the disciples took place in everyday settings. The same kinds of planned or unplanned formative and life-changing interactions can occur when Spirit-filled educators simply invest time to be with students in conversation, ministry situations, and other settings.[2]

This chapter looks briefly at the theological basis for mentoring and then highlights mentoring relationships in Scripture and church history. After that, it describes the vital role of educators in the mentoring process and lists some additional principles for effective mentoring. Finally, it advocates for instituting intentional mentoring programs in ministry training schools.

---

1. Hodges, *Indigenous Church*, 69.

2. Banks, *Reenvisioning Theological Education*, 180–81.

THEOLOGICAL BASIS FOR MENTORING

Mentoring emerging spiritual leaders is based on two foundational theological truths. First, God's trinitarian nature points to the relational aspect of mentoring. God is relational, and our understanding, imperfect as it is, of his relationship within himself is expressed in the doctrine of the Trinity.[3] Mentoring can take place only in the context of trusting and growing relationships that reflect the reality of God's trinitarian nature.

Second, the incarnation of Jesus points to its interactive aspect. Through the incarnation, God spanned the gulf that separated humankind from himself. People could then, at least partially and imperfectly, comprehend God.

> Because humans are created in the image of God, they have been endowed with a general capacity to open themselves to others. Without this capacity, human relationship would not exist. . . . The life of a believer brings reconciliation with God and with other people through Christ. The believer discovers a new dimension of relationships shaped by openness and a growing capacity to participate in a knowing relationship. These relationships include friendship and mentoring relationships.[4]

Classroom exchanges and interactions, by nature more cerebral, clearly have value. However, one should not expect mentorship leading to spiritual transformation to take place independent of more personal interaction and relationship between the mentor-educator and student-protégé.[5]

BIBLICAL AND HISTORICAL PRECEDENTS

A rich biblical record of the mentoring of spiritual leaders exists, beginning with Jethro and Moses and continuing through Paul and Timothy.[6] One factor that characterizes successful, effective mentoring is when it has gone full cycle—when the protégé continues on to invest in younger emerging leaders. This is part of the desired results of the mandate in 2 Tim 2:2 to teach those who will teach others also. Another factor is that most of the

---

3. Oladimeji, "Mentoring as a Tool," 25–31.

4. Oladimeji, "Mentoring as a Tool," 31–33.

5. Oladimeji, "Mentoring as a Tool," 24–34; Elliston, *Home Grown Leaders*, 132.

6. Oladimeji, "Mentoring as a Tool," 14–20.

actual process (shared life, practical ministry experiences, and so on) is much more likely to happen outside the classroom or academic setting.

Jesus and Peter as a Model of Mentoring

Jesus's relationship with Peter is a model for mentoring, and it provides specific ways in which the mentoring process can be the most effective. The mentor should have a vision of where the protégé's faith and practical abilities to become a spiritual leader need to go. The mentor should know the protégé well enough to challenge him or her in this process and in specific instances where this growth process is to occur. The mentor must also consistently demonstrate the desired qualities for the protégé. These aspects of the relationship imply a lengthy period of time, just as it took three years for Jesus and Peter.[7]

Paul and Timothy as a Model of Mentoring

Paul's mentoring process for Timothy provides a longer time frame.[8] Timothy joined Paul's ministry team at Paul's request and with a strong endorsement from his church leadership (Acts 16:1–3). He first served as a learner and team member, then as a colleague in ministry. Paul appears to have apprenticed him through a process of increasing observation, participation, and responsibility in ministry. Along with that, Paul placed a high priority on the formation and development of observable Christlike character traits. He also recognized the work of the Spirit in the process as a vital ingredient.

One side note that should be mentioned in Paul's relationship with Timothy is that the mentoring process is not limited to the season of formal training. Young pastors, recently graduated from training programs, will benefit greatly from older, more experienced pastors who take time to invest in them. Some of the specific areas where older mentors can provide significant help are in forming a ministry philosophy, developing interpersonal and ministry skills, and establishing accountability on a personal and professional level.[9]

---

7. See Cagle, "Renewal through Mentoring," 4–7.

8. Tucker, *Pacesetter*, 23; see also ch. 6 in this book, "The Training Process in Scripture."

9. See Gonlag, "Relationships That Transform."

Mentoring in Church History

Throughout church history, many significant advances have resulted from leaders who invested themselves in the future by mentoring those who would eventually take their place. The best known are the apostle John and Polycarp; Bishop Ambrose of Milan and Saint Augustine; Clement of Alexandria and Origen; Martin Luther and Philip Melanchthon; and John Wesley, who mentored several others who continued to provide oversight and leadership to the Methodist movement after his death.[10]

A Twentieth-Century Example: Rodrigo Esperanza

Rodrigo Esperanza was the first general superintendent of the Philippines Assemblies of God (PGCAG).[11] Rosanny Engcoy studied his life and cites numerous stories and interviews, most notably with former long-time Southern Tagalog District Council (STDC) Superintendent Anacleto Lobarbio. Lobarbio emphasizes Esperanza's intentional personal investment in his students' lives and how he consistently modeled for them the characteristics of an effective pastor.[12]

In concluding her dissertation, Engcoy urges:

> I also recommend that studies be made of the influence exerted by regional Bible schools on the kind of ministers leading the denomination. It is common knowledge that character and values are more caught than taught. Esperanza dedicated much of his time and effort to mentoring Bible school students, knowing that they were the future leaders of the denomination. Studies could show whether intentional mentoring is going on in the Bible schools and, if so, what character and values are being passed on. Bible school faculty recognize that every student they teach will teach many more, whether for good or bad. Such a grave responsibility necessitates intentional study.[13]

This appeal is pertinent to all ministerial training institutions. The predecessors of today's schools tended to focus primarily on developing skills, imparting knowledge, and encouraging zeal in the lives of their

10. Oladimeji, "Mentoring as a Tool," 20–21.

11. Engcoy, "Laying the Foundation."

12. Engcoy, "Laying the Foundation," 116.

13. Engcoy, "Laying the Foundation," 219.

students. All these are vital. However, institutions must also provide the intentional facilitation of character transformation and spiritual formation. This priority of transformation and formation is reflected in Paul's list of qualifications for a spiritual leader in 1 Tim 3:2–7.[14]

UNDERSTANDING MENTORING

There is much more that can and must be said about mentoring in the formation of spiritual leaders than what I have space here to say. Thus, I will highlight only a few issues. My hope is to stimulate educators to prayerfully discuss and consider how they might incorporate mentoring into their training process.

A number of dynamics are at work in effective mentoring. First, it is "the process where a person with a serving, giving, encouraging attitude (the mentor) sees leadership potential in a still-to-be-developed person (the protégé) and is able to promote or otherwise significantly influence the protégé toward the realization of potential."[15] It can also involve the ability to see and facilitate the development of leadership potential in individuals who may be prone to mistakes and who may have challenging personal characteristics.[16]

Second, mentoring is the carrying out of a God-given responsibility that existing leaders have toward emerging leaders. As existing leaders cooperate with the Holy Spirit in this process, they empower and equip emerging leaders to attain the fruitfulness and effectiveness that God has ordained for them.[17]

Third, mentoring is more than just training people or helping them to develop skills or knowledge. It is working together with the protégés "to shape who they are on a deep level of personal identification" by guiding protégés through a process of self-awareness, gap identification, observational training, and controlled empowerment, so that they ultimately become strategic mentors of others. "Ultimately, mentorship is a partnership. It is an agreement the mentor will invest everything she has into the

---

14. See the charts in ch. 5 of this book, "The Development of Spiritual Leaders."

15. F. Clinton, *Making of a Leader*, 248.

16. F. Clinton, *Making of a Leader*, 131.

17. Elliston, *Home Grown Leaders*, 124–36.

mentee's success, while the mentee agrees to work hard and implement everything received to ensure success."[18]

Fourth, mentoring is and requires relationship. "Effective mentoring involves a personal relationship between the mentor and the protégé, which eventually prepares the pupil (the person being mentored) for leadership within the church."[19]

Mentoring in the context of training Spirit-filled leaders for the local church can be described as a vital part of the sequence of experiences through which a spiritual leader is formed. It is a process that is

1. Visionary: the mentor discerns the potential in the current life of the protégé, along with desired ultimate outcomes;

2. Relational: a relationship exists and grows between the older, more experienced, qualified mentor and the younger student or protégé;

3. Transformational: the entire process is superintended and energized by the Holy Spirit.

Using Negatives in the Mentoring Process

Failure is sometimes seen as a disqualification for leadership and not as an opportunity to grow toward becoming a better leader. It is also seen as a reason for not being accepted into a ministry training program.[20] Bruce Avolio argues for discerning the difference between what he describes as recoverable and non-recoverable mistakes:

> You cannot explore without making some mistakes. There is no map clear enough or detailed enough that will provide you with clear milestones and directions, especially when we are charting through unexplored waters. Getting people to be willing to experience mistakes is something that you must do if you are going to create an innovative, adaptive, and resilient culture.[21]

Mentors must assume that their protégés will make mistakes[22] and should be able to motivate them to work through the emotional, spiritual,

18. Pardekooper, *Millennial Leadership*, 139–42.

19. Oladimeji, "Mentoring as a Tool," 5.

20. Banks, *Reenvisioning Theological Education*, 192–93.

21. Avolio, *Leadership Development in Balance*, 113–14.

22. Conserman, "Assessment of Ministry Formation," 58–59. The need for mentoring

and practical aftermath of failure. This shows the student that mistakes, misunderstandings, and other negative or undesirable experiences are a natural part of growth and not to be ignored, excused, or by default allowed to disqualify from leadership.[23] At the same time, the mentor must balance frankness in discussing these issues with an empathetic understanding of the student.[24]

Additional Mentoring Principles

Although mentors are commonly thought of in individualistic terms—and Jesus was an individual mentor—mentoring for the purpose of ministerial training is sometimes best understood as communal rather than individual. At the same time, there are aspects of mentorship that focus on the individual and one-on-one dynamics.[25]

Mentors can affirm their students' growth and progress. Mentors recognize that both they and the students have benefited through this process, and that others in coming years and decades will be positively affected because of the challenges students have met and grown through during the season of mentorship.[26] Mentoring is most productive when it involves a practical goal to meet or task to accomplish.[27] Without a tangible or measurable real-world application, mentoring can lose much of its potential effectiveness.

Mentoring is not optional. The quality of a renewal movement's ministry and its future depend on effectively mentoring the next generation of leaders. For example, Babatunde Oladimeji is a minister with the Redeemed Christian Church of God (RCCG) in Nigeria. He contends:

> If the young leaders that form the next generation of ministers do not experience effective mentoring, then their development will be marginal. This lack of development eventually will affect

---

seems logically to point to the likelihood that mistakes are being and will be made.

23. Avolio, *Leadership Development in Balance*, 113–14.

24. See Cagle, "Renewal through Mentoring," 8.

25. Alvarez, "Distinctives of Pentecostal Education," 287. See Cagle, "Renewal through Mentoring," 7.

26. See Cagle, "Renewal through Mentoring," 4–7.

27. See Cagle, "Renewal through Mentoring," 9.

leadership succession and possibly lead to the decline of the RCCG and perhaps even Christianity in Nigeria.[28]

There is much more that could be added to a discussion of how mentoring can increase the effectiveness of the ministry training course. However, it is also important to consider the significant benefits that can result from the school investing its resources in an intentional, embedded mentoring process.

BENEFITS OF MENTORING

Mentors benefit their students in specific ways. They selflessly provide and point to resources that can help students excel and even surpass them. By modeling expertise, mentors also challenge students to progress and excel. Additionally, mentors work with students to increase their self-assurance, prestige, and believability.[29]

Mentors also increase the likelihood that their protégés will reach the goals God is revealing to them in their season of training. A principal responsibility of the mentor is to help the student understand and advance toward his or her God-given vision for the future. The mentor then empowers the student by imparting the information, abilities, and underlying principles that will enable him or her to reach that vision.[30]

INSTITUTIONALIZING MENTORING

Esperanza did on a personal and informal level what Engcoy advocates on a corporate level in Spirit-filled ministerial training. A snapshot of Jesus's ministry in Mark 8–10 demonstrates that Jesus's toolbox of teaching modalities included mentoring.[31] While mentoring is often understood as an interaction between two individuals, it can also be seen as an interaction involving a number of different people in various contexts over an extended period of time.[32]

---

28. Oladimeji, "Mentoring as a Tool," 3–4.

29. Oladimeji, "Mentoring as a Tool," 49–50.

30. Oladimeji, "Mentoring as a Tool," 54–55.

31. Banks, *Reenvisioning Theological Education*, 104–6.

32. See Cagle, "Renewal Through Mentoring." Because mentoring is relational, it can be done best in the context of the students' experience outside the classroom and as a

Mentoring will prove the most helpful if it is instituted as a formal part of the training process. A mentoring program requires at least four characteristics:

1. A biblical-theological foundation to provide the rationale;

2. A process and structure that allow the Holy Spirit to work freely and individually in students' lives;

3. The context of a community that causes it to be the most effective;

4. A process that leads to practical results and applications.

Although mentoring should be built into the structure of a training program, it must not be understood as limited to planned or scheduled events or processes. This kind of thinking would compartmentalize it and limit its potential. Mentoring and mentoring relationships should also be encouraged to occur in spontaneous and unplanned ways.

CONCLUSION

Mentoring is not the magic bullet that will guarantee ideal or perfect results for a ministry training program. However, it has been a missing part of the training process in many schools. Mentoring is admittedly an expensive investment for educators to make in terms of time, energy, and spiritual resources. However, when it has been done well in the past, it has had a powerful and positive long-term impact on the lives of emerging leaders and those whom they have served. The potential benefits of an informed, competent, intentional, and Spirit-driven mentoring program embedded in the training process will bring great, timely, and timeless blessings to God's work at the local church level.

---

cooperative, intentional process between the school and the church, where each student is involved.

Unit 4: The Twenty-First Century

Chapter 11

Leadership Development in Church History

INTRODUCTION

DEVELOPMENT OF THE NEXT generation of emerging leaders was a priority in the NT church.[1] The apostle Paul mandated that Timothy ensure that qualified leaders for congregations be continually provided.[2] Throughout church history there have sometimes been competing philosophies and strategies for preparing the next generation of leaders. No endeavor, including ministerial training, takes place in a vacuum that excludes history. It is important, with the changes and challenges Christian educators face today, to be aware of those who have gone before us in training leaders for God's people.[3]

This chapter surveys ministerial training from the second to twentieth centuries, highlighting the centuries since the Reformation. It also addresses the philosophies that have been foundational for the processes and strategies used to carry it out. Because the Bible institute movement of the late nineteenth and twentieth centuries has had a profound influence on the ministry training of modern renewal movements, I examine it in

1. Longenecker, *Growing Leaders by Design*, 73–81.

2. Second Timothy 2:1–2 mandates: "You therefore, my son, be strong in the grace that is in Christ Jesus. The things which you have heard from me in the presence of many witnesses, entrust these to faithful men who will be able to teach others also."

3. González, *History of Theological Education*, xi.

greater detail. Although much more information is available about ministerial training in Europe and North America, the survey does include a brief look at training in various regions of the world.

POST-APOSTOLIC (TO CIRCA AD 500)

In the early decades of the post-apostolic church, there does not appear to have been any kind of formal training for leaders of local congregations. This is at least partly because of the charismatic nature of the work of those who did preaching and teaching ministry. However, as the need increased for local bishops to utilize those who served as presbyters and deacons to fulfill pastoral roles, bishops often gave personal attention to the training and equipping of these pastoral assistants.[4]

During the early part of this time period, the emphasis tended to be on developing character and personal formation (Greek: *paideia*) and virtue.[5] As the second century progressed, conflict with pagan, Jewish, and gnostic opponents, along with the process of the canonization of the NT text, required more formal, academic training.[6] In the coming centuries, many schools of various sizes were founded and run under the authority of the local bishop.[7]

EARLY MIDDLE AGES (CIRCA AD 500–1000)

With the decline of the Roman Empire and encroachment of various invading forces from surrounding areas, the church in the West was faced with profound challenges. It sought to preserve the Roman culture in which it had developed and to find ways to evangelize the ethnic groups it was encountering. Monastery-based training and education seemed to be a solution to these challenges. However, the connection between clergy training and the local episcopal leadership remained strong during this time. Additional courses of study beyond clergy training were in some instances also made available in these monastic settings.[8]

---

4. Rowdon, "Theological Education," 75.

5. See Lewis, "History and Components," 181.

6. Rowdon, "Theological Education," 75–76.

7. Rowdon, "Theological Education," 76.

8. Rowdon, "Theological Education," 77–78.

LATER MIDDLE AGES (CIRCA AD 1000–1500)

During the previous five hundred years, Europe had absorbed many of the invading populations, successfully resisted Islamic attempts to dominate it, and become culturally Christian. Part of this historical process was the practical merging of secular and religious power and authority. As a result, the bishops' attention was focused on many concerns beyond the bounds of local church situations and the development of clergy in their geographical areas.

In the same milieu, during the twelfth century, the university developed and became a major provider of training for clergy. While the first tier of education in the university was liberal arts, canon law and theology evolved into post-graduate areas of scholastic study, becoming "less and less related to the work of the ministry and more and more the route to a life of academic scholarship."[9] While religious orders provided opportunities to learn the practical skills necessary for local church ministry, even these schools eventually followed the university model of education that failed to provide informed and equipped pastoral leaders.[10]

REFORMATION (CIRCA AD 1500–1750)

The Protestant Reformation occurred alongside the Northern European Renaissance. A major influence that the Renaissance brought to the Reformation was its emphasis on going back to original sources for understanding of the biblical text.[11] Additionally, the concept of the priesthood of all believers created a rationale for broadening training demographically and for making the Scriptures more available and understandable to more and more people.[12]

The Reformation introduced the requirement of formal theological studies for ordination.[13] Two features of Protestant ministerial training characterized their reaction to what much of Catholic clergy training had become. One was a tendency to be more balanced between the cognitive and practical sides of the instructional methods. The other was that, although

---

9. Rowdon, "Theological Education," 79.

10. Rowdon, "Theological Education," 78–80.

11. Rowdon, "Theological Education," 80.

12. See Lewis, "History and Components," 181–82.

13. González, *History of Theological Education*, 77.

training was more university-based than under the episcopal model, it was still effective, because there was a closer connection and accountability to church leadership.[14] In fact, the Northern European Reformed ministerial training was so successful during that time that it was in some ways emulated by the Jesuits to increase the effectiveness of their own training schools.[15]

POST-REFORMATION

In England, the training of Anglican clergy was generally relegated to the university setting, and until the mid-nineteenth century, the universities had a poor record of producing satisfactory pastors. Additionally, bishops were insufficiently involved in the process (either by their own choice or because the universities resisted their input).[16] Another broadly distributed issue among Protestants during this period was the tendency of scholasticism to separate theology (as a science) from spiritual formation[17] and the development of practical skills for ministry.

To illustrate, Roland Allen served as a missionary with the Anglican Society for the Propagation of the Gospel (SPG) in North China from 1895 to 1903. Following that, he wrote extensively on missions theology, philosophy, and strategy until his death in 1947. In critiquing Anglican clergy training in China and other areas where the SPG was active, he pointed out what he saw as a deeply flawed system. The focus of training was a small number of young men who were expected by the missionaries to perform well in a traditional British educational setting. Their training prioritized academic performance and intellectual content. Although moral character was one consideration for entry into ministry, each candidate was required to pass a rigorous academic exam. This process resulted in what Allen called a native clergy, functioning in ways diametrically opposed to the culture in which they were expected to minister. Such products of the kind of ministerial training that reflected a scholastic view of education would never be considered qualified or able to serve in their homeland.[18]

14. Rowdon, "Theological Education," 80.
15. Rowdon, "Theological Education," 81.
16. Rowdon, "Theological Education," 82–83.
17. Lewis, "History and Components," 183.
18. R. Allen, *Missionary Methods*, 104–5; R. Allen, *Spontaneous Expansion*, 125–31.

Three models of ministerial training related to renewal movements in the eighteenth and nineteenth centuries emerged. One was the theological college in the nineteenth century. These colleges served both the high church and various renewal movements. These schools tended to be much more closely connected to local congregations and their leadership than the university training programs.[19]

Another was the Wesleyan model of training lay preachers who had risen through the ranks of the band or class leaders.[20] John Wesley developed a combination of on-the-job training that consisted of itinerant preaching, focused personal study through required reading materials he assigned, and times of encounter and discussion with groups of these emerging leaders.

The third was the development of Bible training institutes founded by individuals such as D. L. Moody.[21] While these schools did not tend to have high academic standards, especially in their early stages, they combined intense leadership training with evangelistic opportunities in the densely populated urban areas where they were located.

THE BIBLE SCHOOL MOVEMENT

Many early Pentecostal missionaries saw the need to develop national church leadership and modeled training institutions after the schools in which they had been trained.[22] The schools where they had studied were part of the Bible school movement that began in North America circa 1880 and was in many ways inspired by clergy training institutions founded earlier in Europe.[23]

Like their European Pietist counterparts,[24] the Bible school movement institutions were a reaction to perceived inadequacies in how contemporary

19. Rowdon, "Theological Education," 83–85.

20. Rowdon, "Theological Education," 85.

21. Rowdon, "Theological Education," 85–86. Moody Bible Institute's Chicago campus was founded in 1886.

22. See Klaus and Triplett, "National Leadership," 226–27.

23. Brereton, *Training God's Army*, 55–59. Scores of schools were established, but probably the best-known ones still operating today are Moody Bible Institute (D. L. Moody, 1886), Bible Institute of Los Angeles (now Biola University, 1908), and Nyack College and Seminary (A. B. Simpson, 1882).

24. González, *History of Theological Education*, 95–103.

ministerial and theological training had developed and in the philosophical assumptions behind them. Throughout the final decades of the nineteenth century and much of the twentieth, the Bible school model of training has provided a large percentage of local church leaders in more recent renewal movements.

Bible institutes of this kind were attractive for several reasons. First, they were an answer to the need for masses of trained workers to serve in North America and overseas as evangelists and missionaries. The required numbers of workers could never be supplied through the traditional system.[25] Second, unlike nearly all seminaries of the time, they welcomed women who wanted to study for ministry.[26] Third, compared to the normal training process for clergy that required four years for college and three years for seminary, the process was short, practical, and efficient.[27] It also provided immersion into ministry as part of the learning process, rather than separating students from the constituency they were to serve.[28]

While it is possible to overgeneralize about the organizational evolution of all the Bible schools, there is a discernable pattern among North American schools.[29] The founding stage was characterized by a relatively small student body, mostly in their twenties or older. The school rented or donated temporary facilities and had no accommodations for students to live on campus, and it offered only a limited number of subjects. Outside ministry was a priority for students. The faculty and administration were mostly part-time or volunteer. Academic requirements for admission were not strict, and the school was flexible about students leaving for ministry assignments or opportunities before completing their course of study.[30]

The expansion stage was characterized by acquiring or building permanent facilities and accommodating residential students. The program of study was lengthened, and specialized concentrations were offered. New ways of delivering training were added in the form of correspondence,

25. Brereton, *Training God's Army*, 59–60.

26. Brereton, *Training God's Army*, 61.

27. Brereton, *Training God's Army*, 61–63. A strong belief in the imminent return of Christ reinforced the urgency felt by students and school personnel.

28. Brereton, *Training God's Army*, 63; Hodges, *Indigenous Church*, 60–61.

29. See Wilson, "Bible Institutes, Colleges, Universities," 58–59. Some early Pentecostal schools were apparently short-term and mobile by design.

30. Brereton, *Training God's Army*, 79–82.

night classes, and so on. Creating a doctrinal statement took place, unless one had already been done.[31]

In the stage of moving toward academic respectability, the school began to raise academic requirements for prospective students and to offer academic degrees. Libraries were expanded, and faculty acquired advanced degrees, as the school sought accreditation. This may have caused it to decrease students' outside ministry involvement. It may also have moved from an urban setting to a suburban one and eliminated some ways of delivering training, because of limited financial resources.[32] Many Pentecostal schools which had been established as Bible institutes eventually sought regional accreditation, changed their names, and became liberal arts schools.[33]

Several things characterized the educational process at the Bible schools. The Bible was unambiguously described as the ultimate or only textbook and tended to be interpreted in dispensational terms.[34] Although educators may have had advanced degrees that had exposed them to biblical languages, students were required to use and study only the English Bible.[35] Often inductive Bible study, using study questions, was used to give students a handle for their learning of Scripture.[36] Bible memorization was required, and Scripture was seen as having practical application in the lives of students and those they served.[37]

After some time, most schools began to offer more variety in subjects, so that students could specialize in areas of ministry like children, youth, Christian education, and so on. If needed, remedial classes in reading, composition, and other preparatory subjects were offered. Social science and other more liberal arts kinds of subjects were also eventually added.[38]

---

31. Brereton, *Training God's Army*, 82–84.

32. Brereton, *Training God's Army*, 84–85.

33. Wilson, "Bible Institutes, Colleges, Universities," 63–64.

34. Brereton, *Training God's Army*, 87–88. This, along with the use of dispensationalist and non- or anti-Pentecostal textbooks sometimes created problems in Pentecostal schools.

35. Brereton, *Training God's Army*, 88–89.

36. Brereton, *Training God's Army*, 89. Interestingly, this was the method Charles Parham used to acquaint his students in his Topeka, Kansas, Bible school about tongues as initial physical evidence of the baptism in the Holy Spirit. See Goff, *Fields White unto Harvest*, 66–67.

37. Brereton, *Training God's Army*, 96–98.

38. Brereton, *Training God's Army*, 102–6.

Outside ministry assignments played an extremely important role in students' training experience. These assignments included evangelism, social ministry, outreach to immigrants and other identifiable groups, and involvement with the ministries of local churches.[39] As long as schools kept their academic programs simple, students were able to maintain a reasonable balance between classroom time and outside ministry time. However,

> It is likely that difficulties cropped up with particular frequency when school leaders determined to raise academic standards; by increasing the emphasis on classroom studies, thereby redistributing students' time and energy, they may inadvertently have diminished student opportunities for intensive, meaningful firsthand experience.[40]

Much of students' extracurricular experience on campus was aimed at spiritual formation. Often students came to study but were spiritually immature or unsure about their call to ministry or the specifics of that call; some also struggled with unrealistic or self-imposed convictions about what they felt God required of them.[41] Various relationships, experiences, and processes influenced them and helped them to work through these and other issues with which they struggled. School faculty and administration, visiting speakers and alumni of the school, and the stories of well-known contemporary or historical Christian leaders brought them encouragement.[42] Formal and informal worship experiences, scheduled and spontaneous prayer meetings, personal testimonies, and times of revival brought encouragement, relief, and answers that enabled students to persevere in what they believed God expected of them. Through these experiences and times, their faith was expected to deepen and mature.[43]

MORE RECENT INNOVATIONS

A number of variations have developed in ministerial training among renewal movements and organizations since circa 1940. While it is impossible

---

39. Brereton, *Training God's Army*, 107–12.

40. Brereton, *Training God's Army*, 110.

41. Brereton, *Training God's Army*, 112–15.

42. Brereton, *Training God's Army*, 115–18.

43. Brereton, *Training God's Army*, 118–22.

to list all of them, the following examples show the innovative and entrepreneurial spirit that has characterized these movements.

Independent Schools

A handful of large, independent schools like Christ for the Nations Institute (CFNI) and University of the Nations (UofN, affiliated with Youth with a Mission) have been established. CFNI, founded in 1970 by evangelists Gordon and Freda Lindsay, offers training programs of one to three years, and has created a three-year bachelor's degree program. UofN offers programs from non-degree personal enrichment to forty-eight-credit hour MA degrees. It has not sought national accreditation, but as of this writing is in the process of gaining accreditation with an international accrediting body.[44]

Masters Commission

For the last few decades, Masters Commission (MC) has functioned as a loose network of discipleship and training ministries located in North America and other areas of the world. An online search of MC websites[45] reveals some general characteristics:

1. Consists of an intensive, often residential, course lasting nine to ten months (some MCs offer one or two additional years, and some offer the opportunity to earn credit toward a degree);

2. Offers spiritual disciplines of prayer, disciplined Bible study, and accountable relationships;

3. Strongly emphasizes practical, hands-on ministry of all kinds;

4. Usually based in a local congregation;

5. Serves primarily a single, college-age demographic;

6. Often requires a short-term missions trip.

---

44. "Accreditation," at University of the Nations, https://uofn.edu/academics/accreditation.

45. See, for example, Masters Commission USA (mastersusa.com); MCIN.org; www.chicagomc.org.

Theological Education by Extension

Theological Education by Extension (TEE) developed in the 1960s out of several needs confronting ministerial education in Latin America. During a time of explosive church growth and multiplication among evangelicals there, pastoral training schools were not producing nearly enough local pastors to lead the new congregations. Existing training programs often required students to relocate for multiple years to a physical campus far from their homes.[46] TEE creates, based on local conditions, a curriculum and format in which students, most of whom are already involved in local church leadership, can study at their own pace. Included in the process are regularly scheduled face-to-face meetings between local study cohorts and their instructor(s).[47] Terry Castleberry describes how a partnership between AG churches and their Bible school in Belize has benefitted both entities.[48]

District Schools of Ministry

Another model that developed in the twentieth century is the District School of Ministry (DSOM) model. Many AG districts in the United States have begun to offer non-degree ministerial training toward receiving ministerial credentials through this method.

> AG district and network SOMs combine the flexibility to study content between work and family schedules during the week as well as the structure of required in-person classes on the weekend. The experience provides the opportunity to learn through peer and instructor interactions.[49]

Correspondence and Online

The AG International Correspondence Institute (ICI), now called Global University, was founded in 1967.[50] Many denominations have had similar

46. See Wagner, "Crisis in Ministerial Training," 275–79.
47. See Wagner, "Crisis in Ministerial Training," 279–81.
48. Castleberry, "Extension Education," 82–94.
49. Burtram, "Potomac SOM Thrives."
50. Menzies, *Anointed to Serve*, 251.

programs that offer alternatives to more traditional training. With digital technology, this kind of training opportunity has expanded in remarkable ways. I consulted a number of U.S. ministry training institutions that offer extensive online opportunities for associate degrees through doctoral programs. Following are some of the primary characteristics of online ministry training:

1. They offer time flexibility that allows students to expedite degree completion or to take longer than the normal time for completion;

2. Most or all requirements for a degree can be done online (although there are often some requirements about spending time on campus);

3. Outside credit from other schools can be transferred in, and credit can be given for life experience;

4. Some have set start dates for semesters, so that students can be part of a cohort;

5. Internships are sometimes built into the requirements for completing a degree;

6. Some programs give students the option to include modular class meetings with their online studies.[51]

Throughout much of church history, ministry training has shown at least two tendencies. One tendency is to move toward a more academic and professional emphasis. When this happens, training functions in many ways that are separate or independent from the church locally or denominationally. The second tendency is a reaction to this. Renewal movements have sought to formulate training systems that are more connected, responsive, and relevant to the local church and denominational leadership. Many of the options for ministry training in the twenty-first century seem to reflect the tension between these two views of training.

SURVEY OF TRAINING BY REGION

By far, the most available information about the history of ministerial training involves Europe and North America. However, a review of the history

---

51. One program that did concern me was a master's degree in spiritual formation that was offered completely online. This program is to equip the student to lead others in the process of spiritual formation, but it did not seem to have much to offer for the student's personal spiritual formation.

of training must include as broad a spectrum as possible. The following material is admittedly incomplete and of necessity limited to only a fraction of the information available.

Ministry Training in Northern Asia and India

With exceptions, ministerial training done by Western missionaries in China and much of Asia has historically not tended to be done according to indigenous church principles. Two missionaries in Asia during the late nineteenth century, Roland Allen[52] (Anglican in China) and John Nevius[53] (Presbyterian in China and Korea) worked and wrote to change how their missions agencies saw the training of local leaders. Nevius's ideas were ultimately adopted in Korea, and the church there has experienced remarkable growth as a result.[54]

China

Christianity has been present in various areas and times in China since the seventh century.[55] The work of the Syrian branch of the church in the seventh through the tenth centuries to establish Christianity in Central Asia and China are remarkable.[56] The Roman Catholic Church first entered China in the sixteenth century and was able to train Chinese clergy.[57] Protestant missionaries arrived during the eighteenth century, and the training of national clergy became one of their priorities.[58]

The house church movement began when the communists took over China in 1949. This movement was a reaction to what many evangelical church leaders saw as an effort of the Chinese Communist Party (CCP) to control the existing churches.[59] Since that time, while not accredited by the government, it has provided effective mentoring and much practical field

---

52. R. Allen, *Missionary Methods*; R. Allen, *Spontaneous Expansion*.

53. Nevius, *Planting and Development*.

54. Email from Forrest Spears, August 29, 2020.

55. Latourette, *Christianity in a Revolutionary Age*, 3:433.

56. Lewis, "Church of the East," 125–27.

57. Latourette, *Christianity in a Revolutionary Age*, 3:436.

58. Latourette, *Christianity in a Revolutionary Age*, 3:446–43.

59. Yoo, "Training Chinese," 67–72.

experience to students. The government-sponsored seminaries function more like seminaries or Bible schools in the West.[60]

Korea

Christianity first entered Korea through the Roman Catholic Church in the late sixteenth century and experienced considerable persecution.[61] When Protestant missionaries arrived in the mid-to-late nineteenth century, they included ministry training as a vital part of their strategy.[62] As the national church in South Korea has matured, it has continued to prioritize training for spiritual leaders involved in local and international ministry.[63]

Japan

Catholic missionaries originally came to Japan in the mid-sixteenth century. Over the next few centuries, Japanese Catholics experienced both acceptance and persecution.[64] In the mid-nineteenth century, missionaries were again allowed, and by the first decade of the twentieth century about 20 percent of the priests were Japanese.[65] During the first few decades of their presence, Protestant missionaries seem to have not been sufficiently proactive in trusting Japanese to take leadership. However, with many leaders coming from the Japanese middle class and *Samurai* class, churches were able to eventually structure themselves in ways that were more culturally relevant.[66]

60. Email from Forrest Spears, August 29, 2020.

61. Latourette, *Christianity in a Revolutionary Age*, 3:446–47.

62. Latourette, *Christianity in a Revolutionary Age*, 3:448.

63. Throughout my fifteen years of ministry in the Philippines, I met many Korean missionaries. I am also aware of Korean missionaries serving faithfully and sacrificially throughout the world.

64. Latourette, *Christianity in a Revolutionary Age*, 3:450–51.

65. Latourette, *Christianity in a Revolutionary Age*, 3:452.

66. Latourette, *Christianity in a Revolutionary Age*, 3:455–56.

India

Although information is spotty, Christianity has been present in many forms throughout India for most of church history.[67] During the nineteenth century, the training of national clergy by both Catholic and Protestant missionaries resulted in a higher quality and number of people prepared for local church ministry.[68] A Protestant missionary pioneer, William Carey, along with his associates William Ward and Joshua Marshman, made the training of nationals a priority.[69] Southern Asia Bible College in Bangalore has played a significant role in preparing spiritual leaders for the Assemblies of God since 1951.[70]

Ministry Training in Southeast Asia

Like Latin America, this area is diverse in religion, culture, language, and geography.[71] Roman Catholicism entered the region in the sixteenth century, and Protestantism gradually entered the region beginning in the seventeenth century. Considerable ministry was focused on people there who were from the colonizing nations. In some instances, missionaries had more success reaching those from animistic and tribal groups than from adherents to major world religions like Hinduism, Buddhism, and Islam. With some exceptions such as Adoniram Judson in Myanmar,[72] few serious attempts appear to have been made before the late nineteenth century by Catholics or Protestants to recruit and train nationals for ministry.[73]

Thailand

Alex Smith researched and analyzed Protestant missions in Thailand (1816–1982) and made several observations related to ministerial training there. The training of nationals for ministry was to be a priority for

67. Latourette, *Christianity in a Revolutionary Age*, 3:401.

68. Latourette, *Christianity in a Revolutionary Age*, 3:415.

69. Latourette, *Christianity in a Revolutionary Age*, 3:402.

70. "History of Assemblies of God India."

71. Southeast Asia consists of the nations of Cambodia, Laos, Myanmar, Thailand, Vietnam, Singapore, Malaysia, Borneo, Brunei, Indonesia and the Philippines.

72. Latourette, *Christianity in a Revolutionary Age*, 3:419–20.

73. Latourette, *Christianity in a Revolutionary Age*, 3:429–30.

Presbyterian missionaries.[74] Training institutions were set up and produced workers.[75] After World War II, part of the strategy for renewing the work that had been decimated during the Japanese occupation was to establish a seminary to train pastors. However, younger men (in a culture where elders are highly regarded) in relatively small numbers were recruited to study there, and many after graduation were not equipped for pastoral ministry and did not become pastors. Thai Bible schools turned out more and better equipped pastors than the seminary did.[76]

In reviewing AG church planting in Thailand, Samuel Bowdoin attributes effective discipleship ministry and a church-based ministry training school to providing the most effective church planters and pastors.[77] An issue that determined the effectiveness of ministry training was the level of student involvement in practical ministry.[78] In some areas of the country where new churches were being planted, leaders were developed and trained from among the new congregations.[79] Leaders in the Thailand AG believe that effective Bible school ministry should remain a high priority for the denomination.[80]

Ministry Training in the Pacific Islands

Samoa's first known exposure to Christianity was in 1820, but there was no resident missionary there until 1830. By 1844, a theological college was established, which provided ministers for Samoan churches and missionaries to other areas of the world.[81] The school, Malua Theological College, is still in existence.[82]

In 1969, theological education in this region was going through what Charles Forman describes as a quiet revolution.[83] Training had evolved from individual missionaries spending limited time training leaders from

74. A. Smith, *Siamese Gold*, 27.

75. A. Smith, *Siamese Gold*, 46, 48, 83, 138.

76. A. Smith, *Siamese Gold*, 218–21.

77. Bowdoin, "Church Planting," 50–53, 83–84.

78. Bowdoin, "Church Planting," 119–20.

79. Bowdoin, "Church Planting," 125–26.

80. Bowdoin, "Church Planting," 154–55.

81. Pagaialii, *Pentecost to the Uttermost*, 11–14.

82. Malua Theological College, "Serving the Ministries."

83. Forman, "Theological Education."

their particular areas to the establishment of centralized training institutions. The number of centralized schools expanded during the last half of the nineteenth century and in the years between World War II and the 1960s. Each period was a time of profound change in the local cultures of this region.[84] One notable trend was toward a younger demographic of students, who as a group tended to be more internally motivated to study for ministry than their more traditional, older counterparts had been.[85] Another trend has entailed a greater emphasis on critical theological thinking and less on rote memorization than in the past.[86] Related to this is the trend during the 1960s toward using English as the mode of instruction, which exposes students to a greater level of Western theological perspectives.[87]

> We should not easily assume that the changes represent only improvements . . . . It is clear only that changing conditions have called for changes in the schools and as the old education was well adapted to the past[,] so a new education is now necessary. Skillful hands will be required to guide theological education through a revolution such as this.[88]

The issues that often determine the direction of ministry training, formation versus professionalism, and training institutions' relationships with the church do not appear to be limited to the West. The same questions with which European and North American ministry educators have grappled seem to arise among educators in many areas of the world.

Ministry Training in Latin America

Up until the early twentieth century, Central and South America were under a much greater Roman Catholic than Protestant influence. Clergy education rarely produced a sufficient number or quality of spiritual leaders, although there were attempts throughout the region to train priests and other local church leaders from among nationals.[89] Notable efforts

84. Forman, "Theological Education," 151–57.

85. Forman, "Theological Education," 162–63. Traditionally, students had been selected by their family and church leadership to study for ministry.

86. Forman, "Theological Education," 164.

87. Forman, "Theological Education," 165.

88. Forman, "Theological Education," 166.

89. Latourette, *Christianity in a Revolutionary Age*, 3:349–52.

from Protestants in the nineteenth century to train pastors and evangelists were made by Melinda Rankin in Mexico[90] and William Taylor in Brazil and Chile.[91] Although Taylor (1821–1902) ministered in many areas of the world, he established a network of what he envisioned to be self-supporting ministries mostly in the western half of South America.[92] A vital part of his strategy was to emulate the apostle Paul's pattern of training qualified nationals and placing them in leadership over local congregations and denominational structures as quickly as possible.[93]

Ministry Training in the British Commonwealth Nations

Canada, Australia, and New Zealand may be the most widely known Commonwealth nations. Each of these three nations has its own unique church history and ministry training history. However, the effect of ministry training on the strength and vitality of the national church seems to have been generally positive.[94] Usually ministers or priests from the various denominations representing the immigrant (colonial) population came from Britain at first. At some point, the churches formed their own denominational structures, established training institutions, and provided their own clergy. In some cases, these schools offered training for missionaries who felt called to serve the indigenous population of the area.

Ministry Training in Western Asia and North Africa

Although the Holy Land is located in this area,[95] Christianity has struggled in many parts of this large region since the rise of Islam in the eighth century.[96] The various historical churches have often faced resistance that has hindered their ability to produce effective spiritual leaders. As a result, the

90. Latourette, *Christianity in a Revolutionary Age*, 3:309–10; Rankin, *Twenty Years*.

91. Latourette, *Christianity in a Revolutionary Age*, 3:302–3, 334.

92. Arms, *History of William Taylor*.

93. Bundy, "Legacy of William Taylor," 174.

94. Latourette, *Christianity in a Revolutionary Age*, 3:274–76, 369–70, 376–77.

95. Western Asia (the Middle East) includes Yemen, Oman, Saudi Arabia, Kuwait, Iran, Qatar, the United Arab Emirates, Jordan, Iraq, Syria, Lebanon, Turkey, Armenia, Azerbaijan, Cyprus, Israel, and Georgia. North Africa includes Morocco, Algeria, Tunisia, Libya, Egypt, and Sudan.

96. Jenkins, *Lost History of Christianity*, 45–70.

quality of clergy has sometimes been lacking, due to little or no training opportunities. However, during the nineteenth century, under the protection and umbrella of the various Western European imperial powers, both European and North American Protestant missionaries were able to provide opportunities for congregational leaders of these struggling churches to study.[97]

Ministry Training in Sub-Saharan Africa

Other than the slave trade with Europe and North America that began in the fifteenth century, there was limited interaction, including the sending of missionaries, between the West and this region before the middle of the nineteenth century. Early clergy training was focused primarily on those who would serve the transplanted European population.[98] At the same time, European churches and missions societies often stretched their limited human resources to train people to minister to the African population.[99] A remarkable development, growing out of complex African reactions to the missionary presence and the desire to express Christianity in African terms, has been called the African Independent Church Movement.[100]

Conclusion to Regional Survey

The information here is admittedly only fragmentary. However, it gives sufficient information to provide a sense of the need for training leaders from among those who are insiders in the nation or the culture that is being served. It also raises the question of the ultimate goals and aims of ministry training. In the next few paragraphs, I address the bottom line of what ministry training should prioritize.

---

97. Latourette, *Christianity in a Revolutionary Age*, 3:386, 389–92, 397; Livingstone, *Turkey, Persia, Mesopotamia*.

98. Latourette, *Christianity in a Revolutionary Age*, 3:468–70.

99. Latourette, *Christianity in a Revolutionary Age*, 3:470, 474.

100. Latourette, *Reformation to the Present*, 1437.

ULTIMATE GOALS OF LEADERSHIP DEVELOPMENT

An analysis of the purpose and nature of theological education has iden-tified two competing models of the training of spiritual leaders. These models have been described as the Athens model and the Berlin model.[101] In the Athens model, "theological education is a movement from source to personal appropriation of the source, from revealed wisdom to the ap-propriation of revealed wisdom in a way that is identity forming and per-sonally transforming."[102] The Berlin model sees theological education as "a movement from data to theory to application of theory to practice. This movement correlates with its bipolar structure: *Wissenschaft*[103] for critical rigor in theorizing; 'professional' education for rigorous study of the ap-plication of theory in practice."[104]

Edward Farley explains factors that motivated a move among some denominations and renewal movements toward a return to more forma-tive training in Europe and especially the United States. Ideally, under the seminary model, ministers were seen as professionally trained, having a degree beyond the normal four-year college-level. The view of being an educated minister evolved over time from having pious learning to being a professionally trained religious specialist.[105] As the German university sys-tem was being established, it included the teaching of theology to religious professionals as members of one of the major professions (the other three academic disciplines were law, medicine, and philosophy).[106]

In very general terms, from the third century to the eighteenth cen-tury (with periodic exceptions), the trend in ministerial training has been toward the Berlin model. The Bible school movement in North America and its theological college predecessors in Europe signaled a need for great-er balance in education.[107] History seems to demonstrate that the tendency

101. Kelsey, *Between Athens and Berlin*, 19–20, 22.

102. Kelsey, *Between Athens and Berlin*, 19–20.

103. Information about a subject acquired through observation and experimentation.

104. Kelsey, *Between Athens and Berlin*, 22.

105. Farley, *Theologia*, 6–12.

106. Farley, *Theologia*, 85–88.

107. This is reflected in ch. 5 of this book, "The Development of Spiritual Leaders," which examines biblical requirements for spiritual leaders and how that should guide training processes and curriculum.

in ministerial training is toward professionalization (knowledge and skills) and away from formation (spiritual, personal, and relational).[108]

CONCLUSION

If there is one main practical lesson that can be learned from this brief survey of ministry training in the past, it may be a very simple one. It is also an easy one to forget. If it is forgotten, educators and training institutions incrementally move away from it. The lesson is this: *the church, at both the denominational level and the local church level, must remain intimately involved with the preparation of emerging leaders.*[109]

Harold Rowdon's conclusion to his summary of the history of theological education cautions and encourages those responsible for the training of spiritual leaders for the local church:

> We have seen that there is a long and persistent tradition that inherent in Christian leadership lies the duty to make provision for the future. 2 Tim. 2. 2 embraces four generations of Christian teachers, and Paul places fairly and squarely upon the shoulders of Timothy the task of ensuring this continuity . . . . But in principle, training for the ministry belongs to the on-going work of the ministry. Danger, if not disaster, is not far away when it becomes isolated, and exists as an end in itself.
>
> The importance of training "on the job" is shown by the persistence throughout church history of the curacy method. In-service training is no new idea. Perhaps Wesley's training of his lay preachers is the most thorough-going example.
>
> Another dominant theme in the history of ministerial training is the need for mental training at the highest possible level of attainment . . . . The Gospel demands the very highest of which we are capable. At the same time, when intellectual pursuits become an end in themselves, or a substitute rather than a spur to personal devotion, they turn to dust and ashes. Like every human activity, mental study has its built-in dangers. Perhaps it needs to be seen more clearly in terms of the spiritual gifts which are variegated and differ "according to the grace given unto us" (1 Cor. 12; 1 Pet. 4. 10, 11).[110]

108. González, *History of Theological Education*, 115.
109. Ruthven, *What's Wrong*, 265–68.
110. Rowdon, "Theological Education," 86.

Chapter 12

The Twenty-First-Century Ecology

INTRODUCTION

THE PURPOSE OF THIS book is to encourage prayerful thought and discussion about the training of Spirit-filled leaders for local congregations for the twenty-first century. Sweeping socio-political, economic, demographic, and technological changes began to take place at a greater pace than ever before in the post-World War II setting.[1] Those shifts have accelerated since the end of the Cold War and the beginning of the twenty-first century. Even before the end of the twentieth century, there was a recognizable revolution occurring in theological education.[2] As in previous centuries, renewal movements require leaders who can equip local churches to advance God's redemptive purpose in their immediate communities and throughout the world.

Although it is impossible to predict with any certainty what the remainder of this century may hold, educators must consider the current situation and what kinds of conditions they may face in the coming decades. "The teacher's task is inherently future oriented."[3] This is not only true in reference to the students presently being trained, but also in how to continue to provide effective training in the future. Renewal movements have demonstrated an ability to adapt by devising new and innovative ways

1. See Klaus and Triplett, "National Leadership," 230–32.
2. Banks, *Reenvisioning Theological Education*, 4–8.
3. Ward, "With an Eye," 13.

of providing ministry training. Klaus and Triplett challenge Pentecostal (and other renewal movement) educators:

> While the need of leadership for younger churches is important, there exists an even more strategic question for Pentecostals. Simply stated, how do they form leaders adequately and yet keep the Pentecostal missionary spirit alive to carry out the mandate of global evangelization? With such an agenda facing Pentecostals, it must be acknowledged that educational structures and processes, in addition to the content, of course, work together in the formation of leadership.[4]

No event or process takes God by surprise. The Holy Spirit led the early church through many changes and challenges, most of which they could not anticipate. This dynamic, unique to Christianity, enabled them to carry the gospel to massive segments of the known world by penetrating religious, national, ethnic, cultural, and linguistic barriers.[5] In the same way, Christian educators today, who are responsible for forming the next generation of spiritual leaders, can trust in the Spirit's continued guidance. The church is still called to penetrate new barriers. While its task and message remain constant, the particulars of the milieu where it exists and continues to fulfill the Great Commission continually evolve. If one sees this as an opportunity for the Spirit to work, rather than as a series of insurmountable obstacles, greater things can yet be seen.

John Couch makes a profound observation about the necessity of educational structures, regardless of the demographic they serve or the purpose of the education, adapting to changing conditions:

> Like computers, education needs a system prepared to meet the needs of its current generation—in our case, digital natives. It also needs leaders with the ability and agility to ensure the system is designed, developed, and implemented to keep pace with change. . . . Repairing (patching) and replacing (starting over) education is not the answer. What's really needed is *rewiring*—upgrading our educational operating system so that it better connects students, teachers, parents, and society, and so that our schools can foster creativity and innovative thinking.[6]

---

4. See Klaus and Triplett, "National Leadership," 231–32.

5 Peters, *Biblical Theology of Missions*, 305–6.

6. Couch, *Rewiring Education*, 17–18; italics in original.

In previous chapters, I raised ultimate issues that should be considered in ministerial training, including:

1. Biblical qualifications for spiritual leaders and patterns/examples of their development;

2. Following the formational model rather than the professional model of training;

3. Preparing leaders who can discern the work of the Spirit in their community, then guiding and equipping their congregations to work in tandem with that dynamic process;

4. The role of the Holy Spirit in the ministry training process;

5. The relationship between the church and the training institution;

6. The need to embed mentoring in the training process;

7. Demographic expansion of training opportunities.

The question for those involved in ministerial training then becomes: how do we maintain these priorities as we make the appropriate innovations in the process and content of ministerial training in the twenty-first century setting?

I am not a futurist (or a prophet), and in this chapter I do not try to predict the future. My purpose here is simply to discuss known information and reasonable projections about the future that will affect ministry training based on what has already been said earlier in the book. The areas I address are technology, demographic change, generational characteristics, and general trends.[7] I then suggest needed areas of emphasis, based on those observations, in the content and process of ministry training in the coming decades.

TECHNOLOGY

The relationship between technological advances[8] and the shrinking world[9] can be illustrated by environmental ecology. If an insulated wall separating two rooms with drastically different temperatures is removed,

7. Of necessity, there will be numerous areas of overlap between these areas.

8. Hanson, *Twenty-Four Seven*, 20–28.

9. Hanson,*Twenty-Four Seven*,130–31. The term global village in some ways reflects the same idea.

"the two temperatures are blended to form a completely new climate. In the same way, communication media often serve to remove the walls of time and distance. As a result, formerly separate worlds collide, creating entirely new cultural ecologies."[10] Because of this blending of cultures resulting from the shrinking world, millennials and following generations will likely regard and relate to people from other cultures and areas of the world in very different ways than their predecessors did.[11]

Millennials and successive generations see and use technology in ways that are diametrically opposed to their predecessors. Baby boomer Brandon Pardekooper says they "go beyond learning technology the way you and I do. Instead, they integrate it into their mental constructs that are already tied into how they interact with their world."[12] Digital technology opens up increasing amounts of information to more and more people, thus distributing authority more widely than ever before.[13] This trend can be expected to continue to a greater extent than before.

According to We Are Social, 4.66 billion people worldwide were using the internet in January 2021. This was an increase of 316 million from the previous January. Also, 4.20 billion were using social media as of January 2021.[14] People worldwide are expanding the ways they use and interact with the internet, and the demographics of internet usage are broadening.[15]

A marriage between digital technology and all levels of education has taken place,[16] and the COVID-19 pandemic of 2020–2021 has only accelerated this union out of necessity.[17] Effective use of digital resources can bring a higher level of classroom efficiency[18] and facilitate greater development of ministry/professional skills.[19] However, those involved in ministry

---

10. Hipps, *Hidden Power*, 40.

11. Barna Group, *Gen Z*, 34.

12. Pardekooper, *Millennial Leadership*, 77.

13. Hipps, *Hidden Power*, 126–28.

14. Kemp, "We Are Social, Digital," slides 8–9.

15. Kemp, "We Are Social, Digital," slide 3.

16. Lynch, "Seven Ways."

17. Li and Lalani, "COVID-19 Pandemic."

18. Karchmer-Klein and Fisher, *Improving Online Teacher Education*, 23–25.

19. Karchmer-Klein and Fisher, *Improving Online Teacher Education*, 43–45; Kelsey, *Between Athens and Berlin*, 1–28. Those involved with the formation of spiritual leaders must always be aware of the inherent tendency to drift away from the Athens model toward the Berlin model of professional ministerial training. This assumption is expressed by Karchmer-Kelin and Fisher in their heavy emphasis on evidence-based practices

training must remember that the formation of spiritual leaders is a process that is much more than imparting knowledge and sharpening skills, no matter how well one performs those aspects of training. It remains doubtful that spiritual, emotional, and relational formation can be facilitated through mediated means of communication.[20] How can specific Christlike characteristics be modeled other than in an unmediated context?[21]

At the same time, digital technology does have special qualities that enhance and sharpen the effectiveness of the educational process. These qualities are such that, while in some ways, online education may be considered an equivalent of the physical classroom, these two means of providing education are in many ways fundamentally different.[22] Throughout the coming decades, educators will need to keep abreast of emerging new technologies and ways of applying them. At the time of this writing, there is already a plethora of digital tools available to use in educational settings to enhance interactivity and collaboration.[23]

DEMOGRAPHIC CHANGE

One predicted characteristic of the future that will affect ministerial training is the global population's overall improving health.[24] The twenty-first century is also expected to be one of unprecedented population growth, although it may slow down dramatically before the end of the century. One implication of this is that the world median age of twenty-four years in 1950 will increase to forty-two years in 2100.[25] These realities may lead to an increasing percentage of middle-aged or retired people interested in ministry training.

International migration continues to be a major demographic issue. At this time, the two major nations most affected in raw numbers by this phenomenon are the United States (largest number of immigrants, 40

(EBP), which reflects the same Enlightenment perspective as did post-Reformation European university/seminary theological training.

20. Challies, *Next Story*, 88–113.

21. Elliston, *Home Grown Leaders*, 139–40; Portmann, "Intentional Apprenticing," 54.

22. Karchmer-Klein and Fisher, *Improving Online Teacher Education*, 96.

23. Karchmer-Klein and Fisher, *Improving Online Teacher Education*, 109–10.

24. Pardekooper, *Millennial Leadership*, 95–96.

25. Cilluffo and Ruiz, "Fact Tank."

million, which constitute nearly 21 percent of all immigrants) and Mexico (with nearly 12 million of its nationals living outside the country).[26] Worldwide, the number of migrants is projected to grow from 190 million in 2010 to 334 million in 2050.[27] Because of an expected decrease in birth rates in some areas of the world and population growth in India and Sub-Saharan Africa, a significant increase of migration will originate from those regions.[28] While the United States will continue to have the largest number of immigrants, the number of immigrants in continental Europe's four largest economies (Germany, Spain, France, and Italy) is expected to increase from 27.7 million in 2010 to 56.5 million in 2050.[29] Because of an expected leveling off of the birth rate in Latin America, the major sources of immigration to the United States will become Asia and Sub-Saharan Africa.[30]

GENERATIONAL CHARACTERISTICS

Much research has focused on understanding the various generations present in the world today (baby boomers, Generation X, millennials, Generation Z). This section considers some of the characteristics of millennials and Generation Z. Generations are not defined by clear-cut chronological time periods; they are "population segments that share common formative experiences that result in habits, values and life skills that are unique to that group of people but influence the entire nation."[31]

My observations about generational characteristics reflect what is generally understood from a North American perspective. I take this approach for two reasons. First, space permits only a limited amount of information, and a comprehensive study would fill a volume. Educators must inform themselves about generational characteristics in their own contexts. Second, the ability of millennials and following generations to interact globally among themselves is exponentially greater than that of previous generations. While each generation is still a product of its cultural milieu,

26. Campos, *Migratory Pressures*, 3.
27. Campos, *Migratory Pressures*, 3.
28. Campos, *Migratory Pressures*, 4.
29. Campos, *Migratory Pressures*, 4, 6.
30. Campos, *Migratory Pressures*, 7.
31. Barna and Hatch, *Boiling Point*, 55.

the differences between cultures in this century will in some ways be much fewer than in the past.[32]

Millennials

Millennials were born between 1980/1981 and 1996/2004.[33] Like all generations, their behavior grows out of the environmental drivers that have shaped their worldview.[34] Millennials see the world as uncertain, based on the occurrences of terrorism, recession, and the failure of government to sufficiently care for people. Because of this, they seek security.[35] They also attribute great importance to relationships, based on the high level of adult involvement in their young lives. They are therefore more family oriented and seek older mentors.[36] Millennials are highly optimistic about the future. This is based on technological advancement, being taught high self-esteem, and their ability to envision new ways to solve problems.[37] They seek to furnish holistic solutions for the social/spiritual problems that they see in the world. This orientation leads them to address what they see as root causes through holistic servanthood and entrepreneurial activism.[38]

Writing in 2001, prior to 9/11, Barna and Hatch use the word mosaics in reference to millennials. They are relatively more emotionally resilient and self-reliant than Generation X (born 1965 to early 1980s). They prefer cooperative over individual accomplishments. They see modern technology as an integral part of life, not an additional one. They are much more exposed to and comfortable with a variety in ethnic and cultural backgrounds. They are nonlinear thinkers[39] and are not intimidated by realities or truths that seem contradictory to each other.[40]

32. Pardekooper, *Millennial Leadership*, 99–100.

33. Pardekooper, *Millennial Leadership*, 9; Dimock, "Defining Generations."

34. Pardekooper, *Millennial Leadership*, 51.

35. Pardekooper, *Millennial Leadership*, 53–61.

36. Pardekooper, *Millennial Leadership*, 62–73.

37. Pardekooper, *Millennial Leadership*, 74–79.

38. Pardekooper, *Millennial Leadership*, 80–91.

39. While nonlinear thinking can seem complicated, two of its major characteristics are the assumption that there may be more than one solution to a problem and that there are multiple ways in which to formulate those solutions.

40. Barna and Hatch, *Boiling Point*, 66–67. It is certain that 9/11 and its fallout have had a profound effect on Millennials.

Generation Z

Members of Generation Z were born between 1995 and 2010,[41] and being the first generation to have never been alive without the internet, they are true digital natives. They have grown up in the post-9/11 world with a profound awareness of a failing economy, terrorism, and the possibility of being victimized by violent crime. Even if they do not personally experience these things, they are exposed to them continually on social media and through internet news sources. Many in this generation, especially in North America, live in a post-Christian culture;[42] they must be consciously and intentionally led to cultivate a living relationship with Christ.[43] In spite of the negatives they see all around them, members of Generation Z believe they can make positive changes in the world. They have a strong affinity and empathy for others.[44]

Generation Z college students prefer to serve in ways that promise to make long-term, fundamental improvements in the lives of those they serve. They seek to be involved in activities that are creative and entrepreneurial. Significant numbers of them also "will likely seek out multiple internships during their college years as a means to gain connections, experience, and skills that they can leverage in any future occupation."[45]

Among Generation Z, committed Christians are somewhat more likely to marry and have children at a younger age than other members of their generation.[46] This, along with a greater level of entrepreneurial spirit and career or job mobility,[47] increases the eventual possibility of middle-aged or retired members of this generation being interested in ministry training.

41. Seemiller and Grace, "Generation Z," 2; but the Barna Group describes them as being born slightly later, between 1999 and 2015 (Barna Group, *Gen Z*, 10).

42. Barna Group, *Gen Z*, 24–26.

43. Barna Group, *Gen Z*, 31–33.

44. Seemiller and Grace, "Generation Z," 2.

45. Seemiller and Grace, "Generation Z," 4.

46. Barna Group, *Gen Z*, 54.

47. Seemiller and Grace, "Generation Z," 4.

GENERAL TRENDS

Citing the work of Edward Cornish,[48] Pardekooper describes a number of supertrends that Cornish believes will characterize the future and revolutionize human life around the globe. Many of these supertrends are relevant to ministerial training. If we are not currently seeing them, these interrelated developments will be upon us within the next twenty to thirty years.[49]

The first is technological progress. Although there have been discoveries and innovations that have dramatically transformed life in the past, (for example, the printing press and the assembly line), these have been gradual and have often not directly related to each other. However, the coming technological advances will be in "cybernetics, biotechnology, and nanotechnology. We are seeing artificial intelligence—like Apple's Siri and Amazon's Alexa—gaining viability in our daily lives even today."[50] In addition to this, quantum computing will soon make binary computing obsolete.[51] All these developments will likely have an influence on ministerial training in the coming decades, if not immediately.

Sustained worldwide economic growth, especially in India and China, will be another supertrend. This growth will be related to coming technological developments. One possible effect of this process is that the U.S. economy will no longer be the largest individual economy in the world.[52]

An additional supertrend will be improving health. This will lead to expanding life spans, increasing quality of life and health for the elderly and raising the median age worldwide. This may create potential negatives related to overpopulation in some areas and growing competition in some employment sectors. However, ministry opportunities to and for seniors and motivation for seniors to seek ministry training will also increase.[53]

Domestic and international travel is easier, faster, and more economical than it has ever been in history. This supertrend, increasing mobility, is motivating growing numbers of people to travel for education and pleasure. While this benefit is tempered by an accompanying rise in the risks of

---

48. Cornish, *Futuring*.

49. Pardekooper, *Millennial Leadership*, 104.

50. Pardekooper, *Millennial Leadership*, 93.

51. Pardekooper, *Millennial Leadership*, 93–94.

52. Pardekooper, *Millennial Leadership*, 94–95.

53. Pardekooper, *Millennial Leadership*, 95–96.

terrorism, disease, and syndicated crime, some expect the travel industry to become one of the top industries in the twenty-first century.[54]

Deculturation is the breakdown of the factors that give people a sense of identity and belonging. Historically, physical proximity, language, and shared community values have provided cultural identity. For many reasons, including migration, ease of travel, and instant digital communications, increasing levels of deculturation have become a supertrend. This can have both positive and negative effects for the general population.[55] Negatively, existing racial divides could deepen as diverse demographics come into closer proximity digitally and geographically. Positively, greater levels of interaction can lead to more mutual empathy and identification, facilitating greater efforts to work cooperatively toward shared goals and desired outcomes.

AREAS OF EMPHASIS IN CONTENT AND PRACTICE

Technological, demographic, and various other changes have occurred throughout church history. Most of these changes have taken place at a much more gradual pace than the ones discussed in this chapter. Throughout its history, the church and its mechanisms for developing leadership have adapted—consciously or subconsciously—to those changes. These adaptations have been a mix of positive and negative. In the twenty-first century, many of the changes that educators face are profound and rapid. They call for adaptations that are Spirit-led, proactive, faith-filled, and visionary. I suggest the following responses to various anticipated changes, in hopes of stimulating educators to consider appropriate adaptations and innovations.

Respond to Migration and Other Demographic Trends

International migration is expected to increase, until at least 2050. While ministry training for Hispanics in the United States should continue to prepare leaders for that demographic and others that it is reaching, educators should also strategize about how to be ready for an increasing number of potential students among immigrants from Asia (especially India) and

54. Pardekooper, *Millennial Leadership,* 97–98.
55. Pardekooper, *Millennial Leadership,* 99–100.

Sub-Saharan Africa. With strong Christian influence in various areas of India and rapid church growth in Sub-Saharan Africa, educators should aim to recruit students from among the immigrants coming from these regions. Opportunities like this are not limited to North America or the West. Denominational and local church leadership should be aware of these trends in their areas and strategize accordingly. If educators will also do these things, they can serve the church by providing pastors and other local church leaders to reach the immigrants and the general population in their areas.[56]

Generational changes related to marriage, family, and work are issues that may have a profound effect on some aspects of ministry training in the twenty-first century. As noted earlier, millennials and members of Generation Z tend to wait longer to marry and have children. They are also more likely to see job and career transition as a natural and even desired part of adult life. Therefore, training institutions will need to intentionally expand ways of offering study opportunities to potential students from these and following generations. The average age for single students who want to study full-time may trend upward. This will be true of those who study in a traditional campus setting and of those who choose a hybrid online program of study.

Opportunities for mentoring and internships at the undergraduate level of education have traditionally been offered as one specific opportunity during the last two years of a bachelor's degree program. Emerging generations in this century appear to value and even seek out the input of their elders more than previous generations. They also tend to possess an entrepreneurial spirit.

In very general terms, the demographic characteristics of twenty-first-century ministry training students seem to be trending toward older, single individuals. They are characterized by entrepreneurism, practicality, a holistic view of addressing challenges, and openness to input from educators and mentors. Ministry training institutions must recognize and value these characteristics in the content and process of their training regimen.

56. González, *History of Theological Education*, 134–36.

Maximize the Use of Technology

A pre-COVID (2017) review was done of studies of digital technology and student engagement in the college and university setting.[57] This review focused on student engagement or participation in the use of digital technologies with the understanding that engagement is a prerequisite for learning. Digital games, which are analogous to applying learned content to real-life situations, were found to have the greatest positive influence on student engagement.[58] Facebook and various web conferencing software programs were also seen as facilitating engagement, Facebook because of its familiarity to students and web conferencing because of its many features that encourage collaboration and communication.[59]

While it is premature to draw any final conclusions about the effectiveness of digital technology,[60] it does seem to have a lot of potential for facilitating student engagement by providing "authentic and integrated learning experiences" for the learning process.[61] With educational institutions being forced by the COVID-19 virus to rely much more on digital education, the digital technology aspect of ministerial training is growing in relevance as this book is being written.[62] It is vital for ministry training institutions to help instructors to understand how to use digital technology; it is even more vital that instructors remain aware of the potential and limitations of digital educational technology.

Strengthen the Church-School Relationship

One of the core deficiencies of Western theology has sometimes been the lack of emphasis on ecclesiology and its profound, indissoluble relationship with mission.[63] A result of the lack of engagement between these areas of theology has resulted in the training of church leaders unprepared to lead their congregations in carrying forward God's redemptive mission in the world. Ministerial training among Pentecostals and other renewal

---

57. Schindler et al., "Computer-Based Technology."
58. Schindler et al., "Computer-Based Technology," 16.
59. Schindler et al., "Computer-Based Technology," 17.
60. Schindler et al., "Computer-Based Technology," 19.
61. Schindler et al., "Computer-Based Technology," 21.
62. Gonzalez, "Six Ed Tech Tools."
63. Siew, "Theological Education in Asia," 63–64.

movements has often acted as a corrective to this disconnect.[64] The relationship between ecclesiology and mission must be a strong emphasis of ministerial training.

In the past, Western theological education has characteristically been the default paradigm for theological education throughout the world.[65] In general terms, the characteristics of Western theological education in recent centuries have been "a clear church-school dichotomy and a curriculum divided into four distinct domains: biblical studies, theology, church history, and practical theology."[66] Besides the possibility of its being irrelevant to needs and situations in Asia (and other non-Western settings), continuing to uncritically borrow this paradigm demotivates Spirit-driven ingenuity and creativity among spiritual leaders and educators outside North America. The result is that a more vibrant and expanding church than the one that currently exists in the West is taking its cues on how to function from the church in the West.[67] In the twenty-first century, a strong partnership between the church and training institution is essential. This partnership must be the hermeneutical context for forming new training processes and content and for making any needed modifications to existing ones.[68]

I have made the point elsewhere that the local church must be actively and intentionally involved in preparing potential ministerial students to respond to a call to ministry and for their season of study at a training institution.[69] One way technology can serve this purpose is to make young people more aware of the need for and possibilities of cross-cultural ministry.[70]

Creating and maintaining the economic sustainability of training institutions remains vital. Historically, much of the financial assistance for schools located in developing nations has come either from the West or from other economically stronger nations in the region. It is easy for such arrangements to result in an unhealthy dependence (not always limited to economic dependence) on outside sources and influences. With an anticipated worldwide economic upswing, the importance of a strong and

---

64. Alvarez, "Distinctives of Pentecostal Education," 286.

65. González, *History of Theological Education*, 120.

66. See Siew, "Theological Education in Asia," 67 (note); Hipps, *Hidden Power*, 69.

67. See Siew, "Theological Education in Asia," 58–60.

68. Warrington, "Pentecostal Theological Education."

69. See ch. 2 in this book, "The Church and the Training Institution."

70. Barna Group, *Gen Z*, 68–69.

healthy relationship between the school and the national church at the local and denominational levels becomes even more apparent.

OTHER NEEDED AREAS OF EMPHASIS

Shortly before the end of the twentieth century, Ted Ward described the agenda for Christians in terms of applying the gospel's prescription for ethnic strife and division; being agents of reconciliation vertically with God and horizontally with each other; making the Christian education enterprise more relevant and effective; making the formal educational experience a foundation for lifelong learning; teaching students, especially those called to spiritual leadership, to think theologically; and expressing faith in practical ways.[71] These areas of emphasis are relevant to the supertrends and other anticipated changes of the twenty-first century. Ethnic strife and racism are bottom-line theological issues; deculturation and migration will bring it to the forefront worldwide. Those called to lead the local church must be formed into people who can lead this process of reconciling humans to one another based on reconciliation with God in Christ.

Discipleship (being and making disciples) is at the center of the church's identity and mission. While there may be nuanced differences between mentoring, spiritual formation, and discipleship, the preparation of spiritual leaders for the local church is a logical extension of the discipleship mandate given by Jesus.[72] The discipling and equipping of local believers for mission must be seen as a lifelong process.[73] In the same way, the formation and training of local church leaders should never be seen as having been completed.[74] The church and school must cooperate and innovate together to continue forming disciple-making disciples as the century unfolds.

A characteristic of the print age was the sharpening of disciplined, rational thinking processes and the increased use of the left side of the brain.

71. Ward, "With an Eye," 19–23.

72. Elliston, *Home Grown Leaders*, 95–96.

73. Elliston, *Home Grown Leaders*, 49–50. He says, "From these words we can see the focus is not just on the mastery of content, but on a broader development in which one is transformed, informed and equipped to function. Again, we must see that the development is more than just aimed at skilled functioning. It goes beyond to relationships and the character of the person. It does not occur in a once-for-all training program, but rather is seen as a lifetime developmental process."

74. Elliston, *Home Grown Leaders*, 91.

To a certain extent, these abilities have been weakened by the ascendancy of images and icons in communication. A major example of the importance of left-brain function is the need to bridge the chronological, cultural, and linguistic distance between the writers and original audiences of Scripture and the contemporary readers of Scripture.[75] The same skills that were developed for this purpose in previous centuries remain vital for those called to spiritual leadership in the local congregation in this century.

Practical application of theology is necessary, for both pragmatic and biblical reasons. That reality, and the desire of emerging generations of spiritual leaders to address foundational issues in practical ways, intersect. This intersection of thinking theologically, applying theology in real-world and transformative ways, and the drive of twenty-first-century students to address causal factors must determine how ministry training is done.

How emerging generations know things, and how they arrive at what they see as credible truth, is different from how earlier generations did this.[76] Since Enlightenment and Reformation times, this has been done in a linear fashion. Students now tend to process and understand information and form conclusions in a more nonlinear and experiential way. Educators must be aware of and understand this change. They must then be able to devise ways to communicate effectively and participate in the teaching-learning process in this new cognitive universe.

The ascendancy of electronic media may diminish the credibility of the concept of a metanarrative that gives meaning to historical processes.[77] If this is true, it will be extremely important to give students a clear understanding of the biblical narrative and of God's redemptive process being played out in the biblical text and in human/salvation/church history.

CONCLUSION

As I was careful to explain at the beginning of this chapter, the information and suggestions here are tentative. Like the early church and all following generations of the church, our knowledge and understanding are finite. Challenges and opportunities lie before us in the coming decades, and about most of those, we can only speculate. However, the same Holy Spirit who has been available to guide and empower the church to fulfill the Great

75. Hipps, *Hidden Power*, 131–33.

76. Hipps, *Hidden Power*, 69–70.

77. Hipps, *Hidden Power*, 68.

Commission in the past is still waiting for us to draw from his unlimited provision. Ultimately, this is his work.

The bottom line in all that I have said in this chapter is that we must keep in mind the ultimate concerns and priorities of ministry training while we:

1. Maintain awareness of changes—past, present, and anticipated;

2. Continue to have organizational agility and dependence on the Spirit;

3. Prioritize serving the local church, so that it can advance God's redemptive agenda.

My motivation for taking on this project is to encourage educators to engage in prayerful thought and discussion about this. I do not have all the answers. As the century continues to unfold, it may become evident that I had almost no answers. However, if this writing has stimulated prayer, thought, and discussion among educators and all stakeholders in ministry training, I will consider it to have succeeded.

Conclusion

ONE OF THE THINGS the COVID-19 experience has hopefully done is give Christians a greater appreciation than they may otherwise have had for their local congregation. Through such experiences, Christians can learn and grow in gratitude for things taken for granted in the past.

The local church remains indispensable for proclaiming and incarnating, through the dynamic working of the Holy Spirit, the truths of Scripture. It provides tangible, objective proof to those in the community surrounding it that Christ transforms and redeems lives that would have otherwise been wasted by sin and its consequences. The local church also serves as a spiritual family for believers, no matter how new or old they are in the faith. It provides transformative teaching, support in seasons of testing, and innumerable ways and opportunities for its members to serve one another and the community around them. It presents the only real, bottom-line solution for the seemingly insurmountable ills that plague humanity.

God has chosen to advance the saving work of Christ in the world through people, who are part of a local congregation, in the power of the Holy Spirit. The key to these elements coming together to continue this life-transforming and community-transforming work in the twenty-first century is Spirit-filled, Christlike, well-qualified, and equipped local church leaders. As Edgar Elliston sums up:

> The process of leadership development is essentially the process of empowerment. It goes well beyond training. Training is important, but leaders are not made by training nor by educational programs. Leaders may, however, be developed, equipped and empowered. One primary responsibility that existing leaders have is the development of empowered leaders.[1]

---

1. Elliston, *Home Grown*, 126.

Effective, Spirit-filled pastoral leadership is crucial to the health and stability of a local congregation. This is the only kind of congregation that can reach and transform its immediate community with the gospel and produce leaders who can be trained to evangelize and plant churches beyond the community's physical, linguistic, religious, and cultural boundaries.

The journey through this book has taken us through a broad variety of topics related to the preparation of leaders in the coming decades. We have taken a look at:

- The Church
  - ○ Its relationship with the Holy Spirit and the training institution;
  - ○ Its privileged place in the preparation of spiritual leaders;
- Spiritual Leadership
  - ○ The Spirit's role in developing the desired outcomes of training;
  - ○ The Spirit's role in forming the elements of training;
- Training
  - ○ How Scripture describes/prescribes the process;
  - ○ The Spirit's role in the training process;
  - ○ The theological necessity for expanding accessibility and how that might be done;
  - ○ The need for intentional, embedded mentoring;
- The Twenty-First Century
  - ○ Ministry training and underlying philosophies in the past;
  - ○ Issues and priorities for the twenty-first century.

I have offered these topics and issues for educators and other stakeholders in ministry education to prayerfully and thoughtfully discuss. Current and future ministry training for renewal movements will determine the health of the church and its ability to carry out its God-given mission in the world. I encourage readers to allow the Holy Spirit to guide you in the process of innovating and adapting to conditions in the unfolding decades, maintaining the principles and priorities that have guided effective and relevant ministry training in the past. May God bless you as you do so!

Bibliography

Allen, Leslie C. "Joel." In *New Bible Commentary: Twenty-First Century Edition*. Edited by D. A. Carson, et al., 780–91. 4th ed. Downers Grove, IL: Inter-Varsity Press, 1994. Logos Research Systems.

Allen, Roland. *Missionary Methods: St. Paul's or Ours?* Grand Rapids: Eerdmans, 1962.

———. *The Spontaneous Expansion of the Church: And the Causes Which Hinder It.* Eugene, OR: Wipf and Stock, 1962.

Alvarez, Miguel. "Distinctives of Pentecostal Education." *Asian Journal of Pentecostal Studies* 3, no. 2 (2000) 281–93.

Arles, Siga, et al., eds. *The Pastor and Theological Education: Essays in Memory of Rev. Derek Tan.* Bangalore, Ind.: Trinity Christian Centre, Singapore and Asia Theological Association, 2007.

Arms, Goodsill Filley. *History of the William Taylor Self-Supporting Missions in South America.* New York: Methodist Book Concern, n.d.

Arnold, Bill T. and Bryan E. Beyer. *Encountering the Old Testament: A Christian Survey.* Grand Rapids: Baker, 1999.

Association of Theological Schools. "Resources to Address the Cost of Theological Education." https://www.ats.edu/resources-address-cost-theological-education.

Avolio, Bruce J. *Leadership Development in Balance: Made Born.* Mahwah, NM: Lawrence Erlbaum, 2005.

Banks, Robert. *Reenvisioning Theological Education: Exploring a Missional Alternative to Current Models.* Grand Rapids: Eerdmans, 1999.

Barbieri, Louis A., et al. *The Bible Knowledge Commentary: New Testament.* 2 vols. Wheaton, IL: Victor, 1985. Logos Research Systems.

Barna, George, and Mark Hatch. *Boiling Point: It Only Takes One Degree.* Ventura, CA: Regal, 2001.

Barna Group. *Gen Z: The Culture, Beliefs, and Motivations Shaping the Next Generation.* N.p.: Barna Group and Impact 360 Ministries, 2018.

Barrett, David. "Appendix: A Chronology of Renewal in the Holy Spirit." In *The Century of the Holy Spirit: One Hundred Years of Pentecostal and Charismatic Renewal, 1901– 2001*, edited by Vinson Synan, 415–52. Nashville: Thomas Nelson, 2001.

Beyer, H. W. "Episkopos." In *Theological Dictionary of the New Testament: Abridged in One Volume,* edited by Gerhard Kittel III et al., 244–48. Grand Rapids: Eerdmans, 1985.

Blackaby, Henry, and Richard Blackaby. *Spiritual Leadership: Moving People on to God's Agenda.* Nashville: B&H Publishing Group, 2011.

Boer, Harry R. *Pentecost and Missions.* Grand Rapids: Eerdmans, 1961.

Bornkamm, G. "Presbyteros." In *Theological Dictionary of the New Testament: Abridged in One Volume*, edited by Gerhard Kittel III et al., 931–35. Grand Rapids: Eerdmans, 1985.

Bowdoin, Samuel Jay. "Church Planting in the Thailand Assemblies of God from 1969 to 2009." DMiss diss., Biola University, 2013.

Braun, H. "Poieo." In *Theological Dictionary of the New Testament: Abridged in One Volume*, edited by Gerhard Kittel III et al., 895–901. Grand Rapids: Eerdmans, 1985.

Brereton, Virginia Lieson. *Training God's Army: The American Bible School, 1880–1940*. Bloomington, IN: Indiana University Press, 1990.

Bruce, A. B. *The Training of the Twelve*. 2nd ed. N.p.: Pantianos Classics, n.d.

Bruce, F. F. *The Book of Acts*. New International Commentary on the New Testament. Grand Rapids: Eerdmans, 1977.

Bundy, David. "The Legacy of William Taylor." *International Bulletin of Missionary Research* (Oct. 1994) 172–76. https://www.scribd.com/doc/120693454/Legacy-of-William-Taylor?secret_password=277ew475vatocopi9b6m#download.

Burgess, Stanley M., et al., eds. *Dictionary of Pentecostal and Charismatic Movements*. Grand Rapids: Zondervan, 1988.

Burtram, Rebecca. "Potomac SOM Thrives During Pandemic." AG News, July 6, 2020. https://news.ag.org/en/News/Potomac-SOM-Thrives-During-Pandemic.

Cagle, Judy. "Renewal through Mentoring." In *Renewal Manual: A Guide for Personal Spiritual Renewal*, edited by Benjamin Sun, 1–15. Laguna Hills, CA: Asia Pacific Education Office, 1998.

Campos, Rodolfo. *Migratory Pressures in the Long Run: International Migration Projections to 2050*. N.p.: Banco de Espana, 2017. https://papers.ssrn.com/sol3/papers.cfm?abstract_id=3095531.

Carson, D. A., et al., eds. *New Bible Commentary: Twenty-First Century Edition*. 4th ed. Downers Grove, IL: InterVarsity, 1994. Logos Research Systems.

Castleberry, Terry Lane. "Extension Education: Training Coordinators to Facilitate Distance Education through the Assemblies of God Bible Institute in Belize." DMin research project, Assemblies of God Theological Seminary, 2010.

Chai, Teresa. "Pentecostal Theological Education and Ministerial Formation." In *Pentecostal Mission and Global Christianity: Regnum Edinburgh Centenary Series*, edited by Wonsuk Ma et al., 20:356–57. Oxford, UK: Oxford Centre for Mission Studies, 2010.

Challies, Tim. *The Next Story: Life and Faith after the Digital Explosion*. Grand Rapids: Zondervan, 2011.

Christ for the Nations. https://cfni.org/.

Cilluffo, Anthony, and Neil G. Ruiz. "Fact Tank: News in the Numbers." Pew Research Center, June 17, 2019. https://pewrsr.ch/2WJzNHf.

Clinton, F. Robert. *The Making of a Leader*. Quezon City, Phil.: Navigators Ministries, 2006.

Clinton, J. Robert and Richard W. Clinton. *Developing Leadership Giftedness: What Leaders Need to Know about Spiritual Gifts*. Altadena, CA: Barnabas, 1993.

Conserman, Analyn Lapides. "An Assessment of Ministry Formation of the Graduating Students of Assemblies of God Bible Colleges in Northern Luzon, Philippines." DMin diss., Asia Pacific Theological Seminary, 2013.

Cornish, Edward. *Futuring: The Exploration of the Future*. Bethesda, MD: World Future Society, 2005.

Couch, John. *Rewiring Education: How Technology Will Help Unlock Every Student's Potential.* Dallas: BenBella, 2018.

Cox, Harvey. *Fire from Heaven: The Rise of Pentecistal Spirituality and the Reshaping of Religion in the Twenty-First Century.* Cambridge, MA: Da Capo, 2001.

Dayton, Donald W. *Theological Roots of Pentecostalism.* Grand Rapids: Zondervan, 1987.

Deane, W. J. and S. T. Taylor-Taswell. *Proverbs.* Edited by H. D. M. Spence and Joseph S. Exell. Vol. 20 of *The Pulpit Commentary.* London: Funk and Wagnalls, n.d.

"Diakoneo." *NLT Interlinear Contemporary Bible Study with the Original Languages.* http://nltinterlinear.com/greekconc/diakone_1w.

Dimock, Michael. "Defining Generations: Where Millennials End and Generation Z Begins." https://www.pewresearch.org/fact-tank/2019/01/17/where-millennials-end-and-generation-z-begins/.

Dragos, Andrew. "What Is Prevenient Grace?" *Seedbed* (blog), Apr. 20, 2012. https://www.seedbed.com/a-primer-on-prevenient-grace/#comments.

Dresselhaus, Richard. "What Can the Academy Do for the Church?" *Asian Journal of Pentecostal Studies* 3, no. 2 (2000) 319–23. https://www.aptspress.org/wp-content/uploads/2018/06/00-2-RDresselhaus.pdf.

Duraisingh, C. "Ministerial Formation for Mission: Implications for Theological Education." *International Review of Mission* 81, no. 1 (Jan. 1992) 33–45.

Dusing, Michael L. "The New Testament Church." In *Systematic Theology: A Pentecostal Perspective,* edited by Stanley M. Horton, 525–66. Rev. ed. Springfield, MO: Gospel, 2007.

Dyer, John. *From the Garden to the City: The Redeeming and Corrupting Power of Technology.* Grand Rapids: Kregel, 2011.

Elliston, Edgar J. *Home Grown Leaders.* Pasadena, CA: William Carey Library, 1992.

Elmer, Duane, et al., eds. *With an Eye on the Future: Development and Mission in the Twenty-First Century.* Monrovia, CA: MARC, 1996.

Elwell, Walter A., and Philip Wesley Comfort. *Tyndale Bible Dictionary.* Tyndale Reference Library. Wheaton, IL: Tyndale House, 2001. Logos Research Systems.

Engcoy, Dynnice Rosanny D. "Laying the Foundation of Philippine Pentecostalism: Rodrigo Esperanza's Pioneering Roles with the Philippines General Council of the Assemblies of God." PhD diss., Asia Graduate School of Theology, 2013.

———. *Pentecostal Pioneer: The Life and Legacy of Rudy Esperanza in the Early Years of the Assemblies of God in the Philippines.* Pentecostalism around the World 4. Baguio City, Phil.: APTS Press, 2014.

Estes, Douglas Charles. *Simchurch.* Grand Rapids: Zondervan, 2009.

Everts Powers, Janet. "Your Daughters Shall Prophesy: Pentecostal Hermeneutics and the Empowerment of Women." In *The Globalization of Pentecostalism: A Religion Made to Travel,* edited by Murray Dempster et al., 313–37. Eugene, OR: Wipf and Stock, 1999.

Farley, Edward. *Theologia: The Fragmentation and Unity of Theological Education.* Eugene, OR: Wipf and Stock, 2001.

Fee, Gordon D. *Paul, the Spirit, and the People of God.* Grand Rapids: Baker Academic, 1996.

Forman, Charles W. "Theological Education in the South Pacific Islands: A Quiet Revolution." *Journal de la Société des Océanistes* 29 (1969) 151–67. https://www.persee.fr/doc/jso_0300-953x_1969_num_25_25_2256.

Fountain, A. Kay, ed. "An Investigation into Successful Leadership Transitions in the Old Testament." In *Reflections on Developing Asian Pentecostal Leaders: Essays in Honor of Harold Kohl*, edited by A. Kay Fountain, 249–79. Baguio City, Phil.: APTS Press, 2004.

———. *Theological Education in a Cross-Cultural Context: Essays in Honor of John and Bea Carter*. Baguio City, Phil.: APTS Press, 2016.

Gallagher, Robert L. "The Holy Spirit in the World: In Non-Christians, Creation, and Other Religions." *Asian Journal of Pentecostal Studies* 9, no. 1 (2006) 17–33.

"Giano." *NLT Interlinear Contemporary Bible Study with the Original Languages.* http://nltinterlinear.com/greekconc/u_9giai_1nw.

Gibbs, Carl B. "The Training Pyramid." In *Theological Education in a Cross-Cultural Context: Essays in Honor of John and Bea Carter*, edited by A. Kay Fountain, 103–32. Baguio City, Phil.: APTS Press, 2016.

Gill, Deborah M., and Barbara L. Cavaness. *God's Women Then and Now*. Springfield, MO: Grace and Truth, 2004.

Given, J. J. *Joel*. In *Hosea Joel*, edited by H. D. M. Spence and Joseph S. Exell, i–xii, 1–65. Vol. 30 of *The Pulpit Commentary*. London: Funk and Wagnalls, n.d.

Goff, James R. *Fields White unto Harvest: Charles F. Parham and the Missionary Origins of Pentecostalism*. Fayetteville, AK: University of Arkansas Press, 1988.

Gonlag, Mari. "Relationships That Transform: Mentoring and Pastoral Ministry." In *With an Eye on the Future: Development and Mission in the Twenty-First Century*, edited by Duane Elmer and Lois McKinney, 208–14. Monrovia, CA: MARC, 1996.

Gonzalez, Jennifer. "Six Ed Tech Tools to Try in 2021." *Cult of Pedagogy*, Jan. 10, 2021. https://www.cultofpedagogy.com/6-ed-tech-tools-to-try-in-2021/.

González, Justo L. *The History of Theological Education*. Nashville: Abingdon, 2015.

Guthrie, Donald. *New Testament Introduction*. 4th ed. Downers Grove, IL: InterVarsity, 1990.

Hanson, Jarice. *Twenty-Four Seven: How Cell Phones and the Internet Change the Way We Live, Work, and Play*. Westport, CT: Praeger, 2007.

Hervey, A. C. *Acts, Vol. 1.* Edited by H. D. M. Spence and Joseph S. Exell. Vol. 41 of *The Pulpit Commentary*. London: Funk and Wagnalls, n.d.

Hipps, Shane. *The Hidden Power of Electronic Culture: How Media Shapes Faith, the Gospel, and Church*. Grand Rapids: Zondervan, 2005.

"History of the Assemblies of God India." NLAG Channel, June 11, 2016. https://www.youtube.com/watch?v=uBvhnHh3I8o

Hoad, J. W. L. "Prophecy and Prophets." In *New Bible Dictionary*, edited by D. R. W. Wood et al. 3rd ed. Downers Grove, IL: InterVarsity, 1996. Logos Research Systems.

Hodges, Melvin. *The Indigenous Church*. Springfield, MO: Gospel, 1976.

Hodkinson, Phil, et al. "The Interrelationships between Informal and Formal Learning." *Journal of Workplace Learning* 15, no. 7 (2003) 313–18. https://espace.mmu.ac.uk/14185/2/Interrelns%20formal%20informal%20learning,%20JWL.pdf.

Hoehner, Harold W. "Ephesians." In *Bible Knowledge Commentary*, edited by. J. F. Walvoord and R. B. Zuck, 2:613–45. Wheaton, IL: Victor, 1985. Logos Research Systems.

Hollenweger, Walter J. *The Pentecostals*. Peabody, MA: Hendrickson, 1972.

Horton, Stanley M., ed. *Systematic Theology: A Pentecostal Perspective*. Rev. ed. Springfield, MO: Gospel, 2007.

———. *What the Bible Says about the Holy Spirit*. Springfield, MO: Gospel, 2005.

Hull, Bill. *The Disciple-Making Church: Leading a Body of Believers on the Journey of Faith.* Updated ed. Grand Rapids: Baker, 2010.

Jamieson, Robert A. R., et al. *Commentary Critical and Explanatory on the Whole Bible.* Oak Harbor, WA: Logos Research Systems, 1997. Logos Bible Software.

Jenkins, Philip. *The Lost History of Christianity: The Thousand-Year Golden Age of the Church in the Middle East, Africa, and Asia—and How it Died.* New York: Harper One, 2009.

Johnson, Dave, ed. *Training Asians to Reach the World: Essays Honoring Everett and Evelyn McKinney for Fifty Years in Missions.* Baguio City, Phil.: APTS Press, 2019.

Karchmer-Klein, Rachel, and Douglas Fisher. *Improving Online Teacher Education: Digital Tools and Evidence-Based Practices.* New York: Teachers College Press, 2020.

Keener, C. S. *The IVP Bible Background Commentary: New Testament.* Downers Grove, IL: InterVarsity, 1993. Logos Research Systems.

———. "Matthew's Missiology: Matthew 28:19–20: Making Disciples of the Nations." *Asian Journal of Pentecostal Studies* 12, no. 1 (Jan. 2009) 3–20.

Kelsey, David H. *Between Athens and Berlin: The Theological Education Debate.* Eugene, OR: Wipf and Stock, 1993.

Kemp, Simon. "We Are Social, Digital 2021: Global Digital Overview." https://wearesocial. com/digital-2021.

Kittel, Gerhard, III, et al., eds. *Theological Dictionary of the New Testament: Abridged in One Volume.* Grand Rapids: Eerdmans, 1985.

Klaus, Byron D. "The Mission of the Church." In *Systematic Theology: A Pentecostal Perspective*, edited by Stanley M. Horton, 567–95. Rev. ed. Springfield, MO: Gospel, 2007.

Klaus, Byron D., and Loren O. Triplett. "National Leadership in Pentecostal Missions." In *Called and Empowered: Global Mission in Pentecostal Perspective*, edited by Murray W. Dempster et al., 225–41. Peabody, MA: Hendrickson, 1991.

Koeshall, Anita, and John Koeshall. "Ecclesiology to Go: Images of a Missiological Ecclesiology." Lecture, Assemblies of God Theological Seminary, Springfield, MO, Fall 2010.

Kostenberger, Andreas J. *A Theology of John's Gospel and Letters.* Grand Rapids: Zondervan, 2009.

Kowalski, Waldemar. "The Role of Women in Ministry: Is There a Disconnect between Pauline Practice and Pauline Instruction?" *Asian Journal of Pentecostal Studies* 20, no. 2 (2017) 147–70. http://www.apts.edu/aeimages//File/AJPS_PDF/17-2_ Waldemar_Kowalski.pdf.

Kung, Hans. *The Church.* Garden City, NY: Image, 1967.

Latourette, Kenneth Scott. *Christianity in a Revolutionary Age.* 5 vols. New York: Harper and Brothers, 1961.

———. *Reformation to the Present.* Vol. 2 of *A History of Christianity.* San Francisco: Harper and Row, 1975.

Lawless, Chuck. "Paul and Leadership Development." In *Paul's Missionary Methods: In His Time and Ours*, edited by Robert L. Plummer and John Mark Terry, 216–34. Downers Grove, IL: IVP Academic, 2012.

Lawrenz, Mel. *The Dynamics of Spiritual Formation.* Ministry Dynamics for a New Century. Grand Rapids: Baker, 2000.

Lee, Edgar. "What the Academy Needs from the Church." *Asian Journal of Pentecostal Studies* 3, no. 2 (2000) 311–18. https://www.aptspress.org/wp-content/uploads/2018/06/00-2-elee.pdf.

Lewis, Paul W. "The Church of the East in the Tang Dynasty (635–CE)." In *Children of the Calling: Essays in Honor of Stanly M Burgess and Ruth V. Burgess,* edited by Eric Nelson Newberg and Lois E. Olena, 111–32. Eugene, OR: Pickwick, 2014.

———. "A History and Components of Pentecostal Theological Education." In *Theological Education in a Cross-Cultural Context,* edited by A. Kay Fountain, 179–98. Baguio City, Phil.: APTS Press, 2016.

Li, Cathi, and Farah Lalani. "The COVID-19 Pandemic Has Changed Education Forever. This Is How." *The World Economic Forum COVID Action Platform* (blog), Apr. 29, 2020. https://www.weforum.org/agenda/2020/04/coronavirus-education-global-covid19-online-digital-learning/.

Lidbeck, Brian W. *Resurrection and Spirit.* Eugene, OR: Wipf & Stock, 2020.

Lim, David. *The Drama of Redemption: Live the Life God Intended.* Singapore: OneStone, 2008.

———. "Spiritual Gifts." In *Systematic Theology: A Pentecostal Perspective,* edited by Stanley M. Horton, 457–88. Rev. ed. Springfield, MO: Gospel, 2007.

———. *Spiritual Gifts: A Fresh Look.* Springfield, MO: Gospel, 1991.

Litfin, A. Duane. "Titus." In *The Bible Knowledge Commentary: An Exposition of the Scriptures,* edited by J. F. Walvoord and R. B. Zuck, 2:762. Wheaton, IL: Victor, 1985.

Livingstone, Greg. *Turkey, Persia, Mesopotamia, and the Arab World 1800–1978.* Vol. 1 of *The Greatest Toil Ever Storied: Reflections on Protestant Mission to Muslims.* N.p., n.d.

Logan, Robert E. *Be Fruitful and Multiply: Embracing God's Heart for Church Multiplication.* St. Charles, IL: ChurchSmartResources, 2006.

Lohse, Eduard. *The New Testament Environment.* Translated by John E. Steely. Nashville: Abington, 1976.

Longenecker, Harold. *Growing Leaders by Design: How to Use Biblical Principles for Leadership Development.* Grand Rapids: Kregel, 1995.

Lowery, David K. "1 Corinthians." In *The Bible Knowledge Commentary: An Exposition of the Scriptures,* edited by John F. Walvoord and Roy B. Zuck, 2:504–49. Wheaton, IL: Victor, 1985.

Lumahan, Conrado P. "Facts and Figures: A History of the Origin and Development of the Assemblies of God Churches in Southern Ilocos Region." DMin diss., Asia Pacific Theological Seminary, 2003.

Lynch, Matthew. "Seven Ways That Digital Technology Is Changing the Face of Education." *The Tech Advocate* (blog), Apr. 17, 2017. https://www.thetechedvocate.org/7-ways-digital-technology-changing-face-education/.

Ma, Wonsuk. "Charismatic Leadership and Human Development: A Biblical Rationale for Pentecostal Education Ministry." In *Reflections on Developing Asian Pentecostal Leaders,* edited by A. Kay Fountain, 285–303. Baguio City, Phil.: APTS Press, 2004.

———. "Tragedy of Spirit-Empowered Heroes: A Close Look at Samson and Saul." In *The Old Testament in Theology and Teaching: Essays in Honor of Kay Fountain,* edited by Teresa Chai and Dave Johnson, 115–31. Baguio City, Phil.: APTS Press, 2018.

Malua Theological College. "Serving the Ministries of the Congregational Christian Church Samoa." http://www.malua.edu.ws.

Mathews, Kenneth A., and M. Sydney Park. *The Post-Racial Church: A Biblical Framework for Multiethnic Reconciliation*. Grand Rapids: Kregel Academic and Professional, 2011.

McGee, Gary. *This Gospel Shall Be Preached: A History and Theology of Assemblies of God Foreign Missions to 1959*. Springfield, MO: Gospel, 1986.

McKinney, Everett. "Some Spiritual Aspects of Pentecostal Education: A Personal Journey." *Asian Journal of Pentecostal Studies* 3, no. 2 (2000) 253–79. http://www.apts.edu/aeimages//File/AJPS_PDF/00-2-EMcKinney.pdf.

McLean, Mark D. "The Holy Spirit." In *Systematic Theology: A Pentecostal Perspective*, edited by Stanley M. Horton, 375–95. Rev. ed. Springfield, MO: Gospel, 2007.

Menzies, Robert P. "Spirit-Baptism and Spiritual Gifts." In *Pentecostalism in Context: Essays in Honor of William W. Menzies*, edited by Wonsuk Ma and Robert P. Menzies, 48–59. Eugene, OR: Wipf and Stock, 2007.

Menzies, William W. *Anointed to Serve*. Springfield, MO: Gospel, 1971.

Meye, Robert P. *Jesus and the Twelve: Discipleship and Revelation in Mark's Gospel*. Grand Rapids: Eerdmans, 1968.

Miller, Raymond Royston. "A Proposal for Assemblies of God Ministerial Training in Provincial Areas of the Southern Tagalog District." DMin research project, Asia Pacific Theological Seminary, 2020.

Nash, Ronald H. *Poverty and Wealth: Why Socialism Doesn't Work*. Richardson, TX: Probe, 1986.

Nevius, John Livingston. *The Planting and Development of Missionary Churches*. N.p.: Nabu, 2011.

Newman, Joe. *Race and the Assemblies of God Church: The Journey from Azusa Street to the "Miracle of Memphis."* Youngstown, NY: Cambria, 2007.

Oladimeji, Babatunde. "Mentoring as a Tool for Leadership Development in the Redeemed Christian Church of God, Nigeria." DMin diss., Asbury Theological Seminary, 2012.

Paffenroth, Kim. "Jesus as Anointed and Healing Son of David in the Gospel of Matthew." *Biblica* 80, no. 4 (1999) 547–54. http://www.jstor.org/stable/42614226.

Pagaialii, Tavita. *Pentecost to the Uttermost: A History of the Assemblies of God in Samoa*. Baguio City, Phil.: APTS Press, 2006.

Pardekooper, Brandon M. *Millennial Leadership: Equipping Generations to Influence a New Millennium*. N.p.: Brandon Pardekooper, 2019.

Peters, George W. *A Biblical Theology of Missions*. Chicago: Moody, 1972.

Pollock, John. *The Apostle: A Life of Paul*. Colorado Springs, CO: Cook Communications Ministries, 1972.

Pomerville, Paul A. *Third Force in Missions: A Pentecostal Contribution to Contemporary Mission Theology*. Peabody, MA: Hendrickson, 1985.

Portmann, Jeffery Scott. "Intentional Apprenticing at a Hub Church for Greater Effectiveness in Church Planting." DMin research project, Assemblies of God Theological Seminary, 2015.

Rance, Delonn. "Fulfilling the Apostolic Mandate in Apostolic Power: Seeking a Spirit-Driven Missiology and Praxis." Lecture, Assemblies of God Theological Seminary, Springfield, MO, Fall 2008.

Rankin, Melinda. *Twenty Years among the Mexicans: A Narrative of Missionary Labor*. Cincinnati: Chase and Hall, 1875.

Rice, Monte Lee. "Pneumatic Experience as Teaching Methodology in Pentecostal Tradition." *Asian Journal of Pentecostal Studies* 5, no. 2 (July 2002) 289–312.

Richards, Larry, and Gib Martin. *A Theology of Personal Ministry: Spiritual Giftedness in the Local Church.* Grand Rapids: Zondervan, 1981.

Richards, Lawrence O. *A Theology of Christian Education.* Grand Rapids: Zondervan, 1975.

Robertson, Archibald T. *Word Pictures in the New Testament.* Nashville: Broadman, 1933. Logos Research Systems.

Robinson, D. W. B. "Church." In *New Bible Dictionary,* edited by D. R. W. Wood et al., 199–202. Downers Grove, IL: InterVarsity, 1996.

Rowdon, Harold H. "Theological Education in Historical Perspective." *Vox Evangelica* 7 (1971) 75–87. http://biblicalstudies.gospelstudies.org.uk/pdf/vox/vol07/education_rowdon.pdf.

Rowen, Samuel F. "Missiology and the Coherence of Theological Education." In *With an Eye on the Future: Development and Mission in the Twenty-First Century,* edited by Duane Elmer and Lois McKinney, 93–100. Monrovia, CA: MARC, 1996.

Ruthven, Jon Mark. *What's Wrong with Protestant Theology?: Tradition versus Biblical Emphasis.* Tulsa, OK: Word & Spirit, 2013.

Schatzmann, Siegfried. *A Pauline Theology of Charismata.* Peabody, MA: Hendrickson, 1987.

Schindler, Laura A., et al. "Computer-Based Technology and Student Engagement: A Critical Review of the Literature." *International Journal of Educational Technology in Higher Education* 14, no. 25 (Oct. 2, 2017) 1–28. https://educationaltechnologyjournal.springeropen.com/articles/10.1186/s41239-017-0063-0.

Schreiner, Thomas R. *Paul: Apostle of God's Glory in Christ.* Downers Grove, IL: InterVarsity, 2001.

Seemiller, Corey, and Meghan Grace. "Generation Z: Educating and Engaging the Next Generation of Students." *About Campus* 22, no. 3 (July) 21–26. http://dx.doi.org/10.1002/abc.21293.

———. *Generation Z Goes to College.* San Francisco: Jossey-Bass, 2016.

Shelton, Brian W. "The Biblical Case for Prevenient Grace." *Seedbed* (video blog), Apr. 20, 2012. https://www.seedbed.com/a-primer-on-prevenient-grace/#comments.

Siew, Yaw-Man. "Theological Education in Asia: An Indigenous Agenda for Renewal." In *With an Eye on the Future: Development and Mission in the Twenty-First Century,* edited by Duane Elmer and Lois McKinney, 58–68. Monrovia, CA: MARC, 1996.

Smith, Alex G. *Siamese Gold: The Church in Thailand.* Bankok: Kanok Bannasan (OMF), 1981.

Smith, R. Payne. *Samuel, Vol. 1.* Edited by H. D. M. Spence and Joseph S. Exell. Vol. 9 of *The Pulpit Commentary.* London: Funk and Wagnalls, n.d.

Spittler, Russell P. "Spiritual Gifts." In *International Standard Bible Encyclopedia,* edited by Geoffrey W. Bromiley, 5:2843–45. Rev. ed. Grand Rapids: Eerdmans, 1979.

Stevens, Marty E. *Leadership Roles of the Old Testament: King, Prophet, Priest, Sage.* Eugene, OR: Cascade Books, 2012.

Stronstad, Roger. *The Charismatic Theology of St. Luke: Trajectories from the Old Testament to Luke-Acts.* 2nd ed. Grand Rapids: Baker Academic, 2012.

———. "The Prophethood of All Believers: A Study in Luke's Charismatic Theology." In *Pentecostalism in Context: Essays in Honor of William W. Menzies,* edited by Wonsuk Ma and Robert P. Menzies, 60–77. Eugene, OR: Wifp and Stock, 2007.

———. *Spirit, Scripture, and Theology: A Pentecostal Perspective.* Baguio City, Phil.: APTS Press, 1995.

Sun, Benjamin. "Assemblies of God Theological Education in Asia Pacific: A Reflection." *Asian Journal of Pentecostal Studies* 3, no. 2 (2000) 227–51. http://www.apts.edu/ aeimages//File/AJPS_PDF/00-2-bsun.pdf.

Synan, Vinson, ed. *The Century of the Holy Spirit: One Hundred Years of Pentecostal and Charismatic Renewal, 1901–2002.* Nashville: Thomas Nelson, 2001.

———. *The Holiness-Pentecostal Movement in the United States.* Grand Rapids: Eerdmans, 1971.

Tan, Derek. "Theological Education in Asia: Present Issues, Challenges, and Future Opportunities." In *The Pastor and Theological Education: Essays in Memory of Rev. Derek Tan,* edited by Siga Arles et al., 79–94. Bangalore, Ind.: Trinity Christian Centre, Singapore and Asia Theological Association, 2007.

"Thelo." *NLT Interlinear Contemporary Bible Study with the Original Languages.* http:// nltinterlinear.com/greekconc/qe_1lw.

Toussaint, S. D. *The Bible Knowledge Commentary: An Exposition of the Scriptures.* Wheaton, IL: Victor, 1985. Logos Research Systems.

Tucker, Tim. *The Pacesetter: Paul, Timothy and the Art of Multiplying Leaders.* Manchester, UK: Message Trust, 2014.

Unger, Merrill F. *Unger's Bible Dictionary.* 2nd ed. Chicago: Moody, 1959.

University of the Nations. https://uofn.edu/.

Vincent, M. R. *Word Studies in the New Testament.* 4 vols. New York: Charles Scribner's Sons, 1887.

Wagner, C. Peter. "A Church Growth Perspective on Pentecostal Missions." In *Called and Empowered: Global Mission in Pentecostal Perspective,* edited by Murray A. Dempster et al., 274–79. Peabody, MA: Hendrickson, 1991.

———. "The Crisis in Ministerial Training in the Younger Churches." In *Theological Education by Extension,* edited by Ralph D. Winter, 275–81. South Pasadena, CA: William Carey Library, 1969.

———. *Spiritual Power and Church Growth: Lessons from the Amazing Growth of Pentecostal Churches in Latin America.* Altamonte Springs, FL: Creation House, 1986.

Walvoord, John F., and Roy B. Zuck, eds. *The Bible Knowledge Commentary: An Exposition of the Scriptures.* Wheaton, IL: Victor, 1985. Logos Research Systems.

Ward, Ted W. "Servants, Leaders, Tyrants." In *With an Eye on the Future: Development and Mission in the Twenty-First Century,* edited by Duane Elmer and Lois McKinney, 27–42. Monrovia, CA: MARC, 1996.

———. "With an Eye on the Future." In *With an Eye on the Future: Development and Mission in the Twenty-First Century,* edited by Duane Elmer and Lois McKinney, 7–26. Monrovia, CA: MARC, 1996.

Ward, Ted W. and Samuel F. Rowen. "The Rail-Fence Analogy for the Education of Leaders." *Common Ground Journal* 11, no. 1 (Fall 2013) 47–51. http://www. commongroundjournal.org.

Warrington, Keith. "Pentecostal Theological Education for the Twenty-First Century." Lecture, World Alliance for Pentecostal Theological Education Consultation, Stockholm, Swed., Aug. 23, 2010.

———. *Pentecostal Theology: A Theology of Encounter.* New York: T&T Clark, 2008.

Whitelaw, Thomas. *Numbers.* Edited by H. D. M. Spence and Joseph S. Exell. Vol. 5 of *The Pulpit Commentary.* London: Funk and Wagnalls, n.d.

Wiersbe, Warren W. *The Bible Exposition Commentary.* 2 vols. Wheaton, IL: Victor, 1996. Logos Research Systems.

Williams, A. Lukyn. *Matthew, Vol. 1*. Edited by H. D. M. Spence and Joseph S. Exell. Vol. 33 of *The Pulpit Commentary*. London: Funk and Wagnalls, n.d.

Williams, Morris O. *Partnership in Mission: A Study of Theology and Method in Mission*. Springfield, MO: Morris Williams, 1979.

Willmington, H. L. *Willmington's Bible Handbook*. Wheaton, IL: Tyndale, 1997.

Wilson, L. F. "Bible Institutes, Colleges, Universities." In *Dictionary of Pentecostal and Charismatic Movements*, edited by Stanley M. Burgess and Gary B. McGee, 57–65. Grand Rapids: Regency Reference Library, 1988.

Winter, Ralph D., ed. *Theological Education by Extension*. South Pasadena, CA: William Carey Library, 1969.

Wood, D. R. W., and I. Howard Marshall. *New Bible Dictionary*. 3rd ed. Downers Grove, IL: InterVarsity, 1996. Logos Research Systems.

Wuest, Kenneth S. *The New Testament: An Expanded Translation*. Grand Rapids: Eerdmans, 1961. Logos Research Systems.

———.*Wuest's Word Studies from the Greek New Testament: For the English Reader*. Grand Rapids: Eerdmans, 1997.

Yoo, Jong Keol. "Training Chinese House Church Leaders: Factors Influencing Leadership Development Strategies." PhD diss., Southern Baptist Theological Seminary, 2005.

Young, Mark. "Planning Theological Education in Missions Settings: A Context-Sensitive Approach." In *With an Eye on the Future: Development and Mission in the Twenty-First Century*, edited by Duane Elmer and Lois McKinney, 69–86. Monrovia, CA: MARC, 1996.

Index

www.ingramcontent.com/pod-product-compliance
Lightning Source LLC
Chambersburg PA
CBHW060340100426
42812CB00003B/1065